BaptistWay Adult Bible Teaching Guide®

The Book of Acts
Time to Act on Acts 1:8

FELISI SORGWE · JOE BLAIR · CHARLES WALTON
STEPHEN HATFIELD · TODD STILL
CAREY FROELICH · FRANCE BROWN · JANET BURTON
TRACI HUBBELL · CRAIG WEST

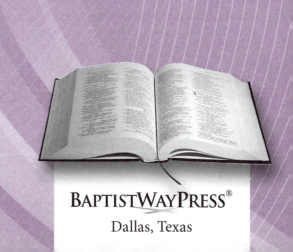

BaptistWayPress®
Dallas, Texas

The Book of Acts: Time to Act on Acts 1:8—Adult Bible Teaching Guide

BAPTISTWAY PRESS® Leadership Team
Executive Director, Baptist General Convention of Texas: David Hardage
Director, Education/Discipleship Center: Chris Liebrum
Director, Bible Study/Discipleship Team: Phil Miller

Publishing consultant and editor: Ross West
Cover and Interior Design and Production: Desktop Miracles, Inc.
Printing: Data Reproductions Corporation

First edition: September 2012
ISBN–13: 978–1–934731–95–6

How to Make the Best Use of *This* Teaching Guide

Leading a class in studying the Bible is a sacred trust. This *Teaching Guide* has been prepared to help you as you give your best to this important task.

In each lesson, you will find first "Bible Comments" for teachers, to aid you in your study and preparation. The three sections of "Bible Comments" are "Understanding the Context," "Interpreting the Scriptures," and "Focusing on the Meaning." "Understanding the Context" provides a summary overview of the entire background passage that also sets the passage in the context of the Bible book being studied. "Interpreting the Scriptures" provides verse-by-verse comments on the focal passage. "Focusing on the Meaning" offers help with the meaning and application of the focal text.

The second main part of each lesson is "Teaching Plans." You'll find two complete teaching plans in this section. The first is called "Teaching Plan—Varied Learning Activities," and the second is called "Teaching Plan—Lecture and Questions." Choose the plan that best fits your class and your style of teaching. You may also use and adapt ideas from both. Each plan is intended to be practical, helpful, and immediately useful as you prepare to teach.

The major headings in each teaching plan are intended to help you sequence how you teach so as to follow the flow of how people tend to learn. The first major heading, "Connect with Life," provides ideas that will help you begin the class session where your class is and draw your class into the study. The second major heading, "Guide Bible Study," offers suggestions for helping your class engage the Scriptures actively and develop a greater understanding of this portion of the Bible's message. The third major heading, "Encourage Application," is meant to help participants focus on how to respond with their lives to this message.

As you begin the study with your class, be sure to find a way to help your class know the date on which each lesson will be studied. You might use one or more of the following methods:

- In the first session of the study, briefly overview the study by identifying with your class the date on which each lesson will be studied. Lead your class to write the date in the table of contents in their *Study Guides* and on the first page of each lesson.
- Make and post a chart that indicates the date on which each lesson will be studied.
- If all of your class has e-mail, send them an e-mail with the dates the lessons will be studied.
- Provide a bookmark with the lesson dates. You may want to include information about your church and then use the bookmark as an outreach tool, too. A model for a bookmark can be downloaded from www.baptistwaypress.org on the Resources for Adults page.
- Develop a sticker with the lesson dates, and place it on the table of contents or on the back cover.

Here are some steps you can take to help you prepare well to teach each lesson and save time in doing so:

1. Start early in the week before your class meets.

2. If your church's adult Bible study teachers meet for lesson overview and preparation, plan to participate. If your church's adult Bible study teachers don't have this planning time now, look for ways to begin. You, your fellow teachers, and your church will benefit from this mutual encouragement and preparation.

3. Overview the study in the *Study Guide*. Look at the table of contents, and see where this lesson fits in the overall study. Then read or review the study introduction to the book that is being studied.

4. Consider carefully the suggested Main Idea, Question to Explore, and Teaching Aim. These can help you discover the main thrust of this particular lesson.

5. Use your Bible to read and consider prayerfully the Scripture passages for the lesson. Using your Bible in your study and in the class session can provide a positive model to class members to use their own Bibles and give more attention to Bible study themselves. (Each writer of the Bible comments in both the *Teaching Guide* and the *Study Guide* has chosen a favorite translation. You're free to use the Bible translation you prefer and compare it with the translations chosen, of course.)

6. After reading all the Scripture passages in your Bible, then read the Bible comments in the *Study Guide.* The Bible comments are intended to be an aid to your study of the Bible. Read also the small articles—"sidebars"—in each lesson. They are intended to provide additional, enrichment information and inspiration and to encourage thought and application. Try to answer for yourself the questions included in each lesson. They're intended to encourage further thought and application, and you can also use them in the class session itself. Continue your Bible study with the aid of the Bible comments included in this *Teaching Guide.*

7. Review the "Teaching Plans" in this *Teaching Guide.* Consider how these suggestions would help you teach this Bible passage in your class to accomplish the teaching aim.

8. Consider prayerfully the needs of your class, and think about how to teach so you can help your class learn best.

9. Develop and follow a lesson plan based on the suggestions in this *Teaching Guide,* with alterations as needed for your class.

10. Enjoy leading your class in discovering the meaning of the Scripture passages and in applying these passages to their lives.

Adult Online Bible Commentary. Plan to get the additional adult Bible study comments—*Adult Online Bible Commentary*—by Dr. Jim Denison (president, Denison Forum on Truth and Culture, and theologian-in-residence, Baptist General Convention of Texas). Call 1–866–249–1799 or e-mail baptistway@texasbaptists.org to order *Adult Online Bible Commentary.* It is available only in electronic format (PDF) from our website. The price of these comments is $6 for individuals and $25 for a group of five. A church or class that participates in our advance order program for free shipping can receive *Adult Online Bible Commentary* free. Call 1–866–249–1799 or see www.baptistwaypress.org for information on participating in our free shipping program for the next study.

Adult Online Teaching Plans. An additional teaching plan is also available in electronic format (PDF) by calling 1–866–249–1799. The price of these plans is $5 for an individual and $20 for a group of five. It is available only in electronic format (PDF) from our website. A church or class that participates in our advance order program for free shipping can receive *Adult Online Teaching Plans* free. Call 1–866–249–1799 or see www.baptistwaypress.org for information on participating in our free shipping program for the next study.

FREE! Downloadable teaching resource items for use in your class are available at www.baptistwaypress.org! Watch for them in "Teaching Plans" for each lesson. Then go online to www.baptistwaypress.org and click on "Teaching Resource Items" for this study. These items are selected from "Teaching Plans." They are provided online to make lesson preparation easier for hand-outs and similar items. Permission is granted to download these teaching resource items, print them out, copy them as needed, and use them in your class.

IN ADDITION: Enrichment teaching help is provided in the internet edition of the *Baptist Standard.* Access the **FREE** internet information by checking the *Baptist Standard* website at www.baptiststandard.com. Call 214–630–4571 to begin your subscription to the printed or electronic edition of the *Baptist Standard.*

Writers of This Teaching Guide

Felisi Sorgwe, writer of "Bible Comments" for lessons one through three, is assistant professor of Christianity in the School of Theology at Houston Baptist University, Houston, Texas. Dr. Sorgwe is also pastor of Maranatha International Church, Houston. A dual citizen of Nigeria and the United States, he received two master's degrees from Southwestern Baptist Theological Seminary and the Ph.D. in Religion degree from Baylor University.

Carey D. Froelich wrote "Teaching Plans" for lessons one through three. He recently retired after more than forty years of full-time ministry with churches in Texas and Louisiana. His passion for ministry has been discipleship, and he has prepared to assist pastorless congregations through intentional or traditional interim ministry. He and his wife Kaye live in Baytown, Texas.

Joe Blair wrote "Bible Comments" for lessons four through six. Dr. Blair is professor of Christianity and Philosophy at Houston Baptist University, Houston, Texas. He has also taught at Union University, Jackson, Tennessee, and served as pastor of churches in Louisiana. He is a graduate of Louisiana Tech University and of New Orleans Baptist Theological Seminary (Th.D.).

France Brown, writer of "Teaching Plans" for lessons four through six, serves as the Earnest L. Mays Assistant Professor of Expository Preaching & Biblical Teaching at the College of Biblical Studies—Houston. He is the author of two books: *Passport to Life: Explore God's Word, Experience God's Blessings* and *Transformational Teaching: A guide to developing and delivering life changing Bible lessons.* France gives leadership to the Christian Education Ministry at the New Providence Baptist Church, Houston, Texas. He is a graduate of Blinn College (A.A.), Texas A&M University (B.A.), and Dallas Theological Seminary (Th.M.).

Charles Walton wrote "Bible Comments" for lessons seven and eight. Dr. Walton is a native of Baton Rouge, Louisiana, and a graduate of Louisiana State University and Southwestern Baptist Theological Seminary. He is retired after serving forty years as a pastor of Texas Baptist congregations. He and his wife, Brenda, have two grown children and two grandchildren. They make their home in Conroe, Texas, where Dr. Walton serves as chaplain of the Conroe Police Department.

Janet Burton wrote "Teaching Plans" for lessons seven through nine. She lives in Austin, Texas, and is widely known for her work as a Christian educator, author, and conference leader. She is the author of two books and has written numerous assignments for BAPTISTWAY® study materials.

Stephen G. Hatfield, writer of "Bible Comments" for lessons nine through eleven, is pastor of the First Baptist Church, Lewisville, Texas. Dr. Hatfield is a graduate of Ouachita Baptist University (B.A.) and Southwestern Baptist Theological Seminary (M.Div., Ph.D.). He also serves as a teaching fellow for the B. H. Carroll Theological Institute. This is his fourth set of "Bible Comments" for BaptistWay.

Traci Hubbell, writer of "Teaching Plans" for lessons ten and eleven, is active in the singles, children's, and worship ministries at her church, South Oaks Baptist Church in Arlington, Texas. She has a master's degree in Communication from the University of Denver and teaches various communication and speech courses at several local college and university campuses. Traci lives in Arlington with her two children.

Todd D. Still (B.A., Baylor; M.Div., Southwestern Baptist Theological Seminary; Ph.D., University of Glasgow) wrote "Bible Comments" on lessons twelve and thirteen. Dr. Still serves as Associate Professor of Christian Scriptures (New Testament) at the George W. Truett Theological Seminary at Baylor University. Before coming to Truett, he taught at Dallas Baptist University and at Gardner-Webb University's School of Divinity. Among his other writings, Still has written a commentary on Colossians (*Expositor's Bible Commentary,* revised edition, volume 12) and a commentary on Philippians and Philemon for the

Smyth & Helwys Commentary Series. In addition to his work at Baylor, he has served Baptist congregations in a variety of ministerial capacities.

Craig West is the writer of "Teaching Plans" for lessons twelve and thirteen. He serves as pastor of the First Baptist Church, Monroe, Louisiana. He has also served as pastor in Arkansas and as minister of music and education in churches in Texas. He is a graduate of Southwestern Baptist Theological Seminary. Craig has written several previous assignments for BAPTISTWAY®.

The Book of Acts: Time to Act on Acts 1:8

FOCAL TEXT
Acts 1:1–8

BACKGROUND
Acts 1:1–11

MAIN IDEA
Jesus instructed his
disciples that they were
to be his witnesses.

QUESTION TO EXPLORE
Whose witness are you?

TEACHING AIM
To lead participants to commit
themselves to be Jesus'
witnesses and to identify in
this series of Bible studies
how they will do that

LESSON ONE

Accept Responsibility for Being Jesus' Witness

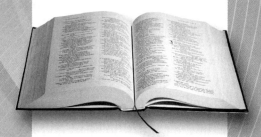

BIBLE COMMENTS

Understanding the Context

Acts of the Apostles is Luke's second book in the New Testament. It is the sequel to his gospel, the Gospel of Luke. In his prologue to Acts, Luke gave a quick summary of his Gospel. Luke's focus in Acts was to give the history of the early church.

Acts 1:3 tells us that the length of time from the resurrection of our Lord to his ascension was forty days. During this time the risen Lord appeared to and taught his disciples. This was a pivotal period for the disciples.

Acts 1:1–8 points out some main themes the risen Lord focused on during this period. The risen Lord took pains to assure his disciples that he was real, not a ghost.

The risen Lord further reminded the disciples that his entire earthly ministry, including his crucifixion and resurrection, was in fulfillment of what the prophets had foretold. On the road to Emmaus, he actually chided Cleopas and his traveling companion—thus chiding all the other disciples as well—saying, "O foolish men and slow of heart to believe in all that the prophets have spoken! Was it not necessary for the Christ to suffer these things and to enter into His glory?" (Luke 24:25–26).[1]

A third theme was that the risen Lord opened the understanding of the disciples. Luke pointed out that on the road to Emmaus, the risen Lord began with Moses and all the prophets and "explained to them the things concerning Himself in all the Scriptures" (Luke 24:27). After the risen Lord had made himself known at the breaking of bread and then disappeared, the two disciples said to themselves in amazement, "Were not our hearts burning within us while He was speaking to us on the road, while He was explaining the Scriptures to us?" (Luke 24:32). Luke emphasized again that later that evening the risen Lord opened the minds of all the disciples "to understand the Scriptures" (Luke 24:45).

The fourth theme was that the risen Lord clearly told his disciples that he was leaving them to carry on a very important mission, the mission we call The Great Commission. They were to be his witnesses (Acts 1:8).

Interpreting the Scriptures

The Earthly Ministry of Jesus Before His Crucifixion (1:1)

As Luke began Acts, he made the connection to his first book, the Gospel of Luke. He referred to "the first account I composed," and he addressed Theophilus, just as he had in his Gospel (see Luke 1:3). "Theophilus" means *lover of God,* but Luke did not dedicate his books to the generic *lover of God,* that is, any believer. Luke's use of the address "most excellent Theophilus" in Luke 1:3, an address that was reserved for high government officials such as Governor Felix (see Acts 23:26), meant that Theophilus was most likely a high government official. It was also very likely that Theophilus was a new believer, for Luke indicated in his Gospel that he was writing "so that you might know the exact truth about the things you have been taught" (Luke 1:4).

In Acts 1:3, Luke stated that in his Gospel he had written about "all that Jesus began to do and teach." This phrase encompasses everything Luke had written in his Gospel, from the infancy narrative of Jesus to the events of Holy Week and up to his ascension in Luke 24.

The Ministry of the Risen Lord from His Resurrection to His Ascension (1:2–8)

1:2. In using the phrase, "until the day when He was taken up," Luke was referring to his account of the ascension of our Lord, which is spoken of in Luke 24:50–53. There Luke had simply said that the risen Lord led his disciples as far as Bethany, and as he blessed them, with his hands lifted up, "He parted from them" (Luke 24:51). He then noted that the disciples returned "to Jerusalem with great joy and were continually in the temple, praising God" (Luke 24:52b–53).

Luke, the only New Testament writer who gave us any account of the ascension of our Lord, gave us some more details of this remarkable event here in Acts 1. Here Luke elaborated that it was while the disciples were looking at Jesus, evidently as he was blessing them, that he was lifted up into a cloud, and the cloud covered him up (see Acts 1:9). He also described the vision of the angels that the disciples saw (1:10–11). Understandably, the disciples were all astonished, and they were "gazing intently into the sky" (1:10) as the risen Lord strangely went up away from them, when two angels, described as "two men in white clothing," stood beside them, chiding, and in a way mocking, them. What the angels said to the disciples is noteworthy. They said, "Men of Galilee, why do you stand looking into the sky? This Jesus who has been taken up from you into heaven will come in just the same way as you have watched Him go into heaven" (1:11). The angels were telling the disciples—and us—that the ascension of our Lord should point us to his Second Coming. The same Jesus who had just been taken up visibly in the clouds into the heavens will return in the clouds visibly some day.

1:3. Luke stressed that the risen Lord used "many convincing proofs" to assure his disciples that he was alive. In his Gospel, Luke had detailed some of these. Luke told us that when the risen Lord appeared to his disciples in the Upper Room and they were startled and frightened, thinking that they were seeing a ghost, the risen Lord said to them, "Why are you troubled, and why do doubts arise in your hearts?" (Luke 24:38). The risen Lord proceeded to show them his hands and feet, obviously with the nail prints in them, and pointed out the obvious, "See My hands and My feet, that it is I Myself; touch Me and see, for a spirit does not have flesh and bones as you see that I have" (Luke 24:39). Luke described the understandable mixed feelings that the disciples had, saying, "They still could not believe it because of their joy and amazement" (Luke 24:41). The risen Lord then did something that would remove their astonishment from their joy. He asked them whether they had any food. They gave him a piece of broiled fish, and he took it and ate it in their presence (see Luke 24:41–43). They were not seeing a ghost after all, and it was no hallucination!

The risen Lord appeared to his disciples for a period of forty days, during which he taught them. He no longer stayed twenty-four hours a day with his disciples. He would appear to them, teach them, and then vanish from their sight. In summarizing the risen Lord's teaching during this forty-day period, Acts 1:3 says he taught them "concerning the kingdom of God." "The kingdom of God" is a phrase that our Lord used synonymously with "the kingdom of heaven" found in Matthew. Further, to enter the kingdom of God is the same as having eternal life. The kingdom of God is where God reigns. It is where God's rule is seen in action.

1:4. The last words of Jesus recorded by Luke in his Gospel state the clear command Jesus gave his disciples, "And behold I am sending forth the promise of My Father upon you, but you are to stay in the city until you are clothed with power from on high" (Luke 24:49). Luke made sure he referred to this command in this brief summary of his Gospel.

1:5. The risen Lord said, "John baptized with water, but you shall be baptized with the Holy Spirit not many days from now." Interestingly, the "not many days from now" would turn out to be ten days. John the Baptist too had said what was almost identical to the Lord's statement, "I baptize you with water, but One is coming who is mightier than I . . . He will baptize you with the Holy Spirit and fire" (Luke 3:16). Lesson two will shed some light on the meaning of *baptism with the Holy Spirit*.

1:6. What the disciples asked the Lord at this time was a clear indication that they had very little understanding of Jesus' mission. They asked him, "Lord, is it at this time You are restoring the kingdom to Israel?" It is obvious that they were thinking of an earthly kingdom. The two disciples on the road to Emmaus had expressed similar sentiments, "We were hoping that it was He who was going to redeem Israel" (Luke 24:21).

1:7. The Lord's answer was his way of saying, *You really do not have a clue, do you?* He would say, in essence, *Let me tell you what you should be concerning yourselves with.*

1:8. Luke was leading to this key statement, the version of the Great Commission in Acts. The Lord told them that, first, the Holy Spirit would come on them; second, they would receive power from the Holy Spirit; and third, they were to be Jesus' witnesses.

The risen Lord then mapped out how the disciples were to be his witnesses. They were to begin at Jerusalem where the Holy Spirit would descend on them. They were then to go to the rest of the province of Judea. Following that, they were to venture out to Samaria and then to all parts of the world. Luke spent the rest of Acts of the Apostles showing that the disciples did in fact do this.

Focusing on the Meaning

The risen Lord said to his disciples, "You shall be My witnesses" (Acts I:8). He did not just say, *You shall be witnesses*. We need to be *Jesus'* witnesses. Are you a witness? If so, whose witness are you?

To be a witness for Jesus is to testify for him. We witness by our actions and by our words. Jesus said, "Let your light shine before men in such a way that they may see your good works, and glorify your Father who is in heaven" (Matthew 5:16). When people see our good works, they are not to glorify us but to glorify our heavenly Father. There are many things people claim to be doing for Christ when they are in fact doing them for their own glory. For instance, is there a point when what we are buying for the church ceases to be something we are purchasing simply to do God's work?

Are you a credible witness for Christ? When an attorney is unable to go after a plaintiff or a defendant, an established tactic is to go after the witness. If the attorney can impeach (discredit) the witness, that attorney can weaken the case of the person the witness is supporting. An impeachable witness not only does little good but actually does harm to the cause of Christ. The devil is very clever in impeaching witnesses, and he knows that. We must lead our lives in such a way that the devil would not be able to impeach us. We would then be in a position to be bold, vocal witnesses for Christ.

TEACHING PLANS

Teaching Plan—Varied Learning Activities

Connect with Life

1. Instruct the class to form groups of two or three people each with people near them. Ask each group to describe a setting in which they are comfortable talking with others and to identify the topic

(for example, talking about a football game, a shopping trip, or a good movie or restaurant). Allow one or two minutes.

2. Now ask participants to describe an event your boss, spouse, or friend has asked you to attend, but which you believe will make you feel very uncomfortable (for example, attending a party where you don't know anyone). Allow two or three minutes.

3. Ask: *What are some of the factors that make us feel either comfortable or uncomfortable in those settings*? After two or three minutes in the small groups, invite volunteers to describe some of those factors.

4. Ask: *In the case of attending an uncomfortable activity, what factors encouraged you to participate anyway?*

5. Remind members that the Book of Acts reveals how Jesus' followers were willing to face persecution—to become uncomfortable, to say the least—in order to be faithful to the mission of Christ. Ask members to read the opening sentence in "Introducing the Book of Acts: Time to Act on Acts 1:8" in the *Study Guide* in the section labeled, "This Study," as follows: "This study of the Book of Acts focus on thirteen portraits or vignettes of what being Jesus' witnesses meant in the lives of the early disciples." Overview the study briefly by summarizing "Introducing the Book of Acts: Time to Act on Acts 1:8" and referring to the table of contents in the *Study Guide.* Note that the purpose of this study of the Book of Acts will be to discover the meaning to us of being witnesses for Jesus and actually to be witnesses for Jesus. Refer to the Study Aim for this lesson in the *Study Guide.*

6. Ask: *How has being a witness for Christ ever been uncomfortable for you?*

Guide Bible Study

7. Enlist a member to read Acts 1:1–5. Remind the class that most scholars accept Luke as the author of the book (see Luke 1:1–4). Tell them that Luke 24:36–53 provides a similar account.

8. Lead members to discuss what is meant by the phrase, "you will be baptized with the Holy Spirit" (Acts 1:5). Be prepared to guide discussion to include both the Pentecost experience (Acts 2) and an understanding that the Holy Spirit comes to every believer. Refer to the quote from F.F. Bruce in lesson one in the *Study Guide* under the heading "Prologue to Acts (Acts 1:1–5)."

9. Invite someone to read Acts 1:6. Ask: *Why were the disciples asking about restoring the kingdom to Israel?* Call attention in the *Study Guide* under the heading "Prologue to Acts (Acts 1:1–5)" to the following sentence: "The kingdom of God is not just an earthly fulfillment but an eternal reality that includes God's covenant with Israel and the church but is the reign of God forever." Note that in spite of the resurrection, the disciples still did not grasp what Jesus had been preparing them to do.

10. Have someone read Acts 1:7–8. Note that Jesus deflected their inquiry about the nation's future by pointing them to the authority of God. Ask: *How does Jesus' answer apply to us?* (When we get sidetracked, we need to return to the plans and authority of God.)

11. Remind members that Acts 1:8 is recognized, like Matthew 28:18–20, as *The Great Commission,* and that it has become a primary motivation for sending missionaries to people all around the world. Note that this verse incorporates four great words that should compel every believer to be personally involved in responding to this commission.

12. Write the words "power" and "Spirit" on the board. Ask members to identify ways that the Holy Spirit makes the power of God evident in our lives. Remind them that it was the same Holy Spirit who enabled Jesus to resist the tempter in the wilderness and in Gethsemane.

13. Write the word "earth" on the board. Tell members that Jerusalem, Judea, Samaria, and the "remotest part of the earth" represent the unlimited geographic scope of the responsibility Jesus gave to the church.

Encourage Application

14. Write "witness" on the board, and ask members to describe what this word means to them. Note that the text shows that the word is a *noun*—it names what we *are* as disciples of Jesus.

15. Call attention to the small article, "Witnesses," in the *Study Guide*. Ask members to read the selection silently.

16. Remind the class of the opening exercise in step 1. Ask members to weigh any feelings of discomfort about being a witness against their love for Jesus. Encourage them to identify just one person who could be influenced for Christ by their witness. Encourage them further to commit themselves to look for ways throughout this study to be faithful witnesses for Christ. Close the session in prayer for members to have an awareness of the Spirit's empowering presence in their lives.

Teaching Plan—Lecture and Discussion

Connect with Life

1. Ask: *How did the story of Jesus get to us today from a small group of frightened people huddled with him near Jerusalem nearly 2000 years ago?* Encourage members to think of the ways the apostles shared faith in Christ, how Paul took the message to Greece and Rome, and how Christians through the ages have been faithful to tell others about Christ.

2. Invite members to look at "Introducing the Book of Acts: Time to Act on Acts 1:8" in the *Study Guide* and to note how the thirteen lessons in this study will demonstrate how the people literally interpreted Jesus' Great Commission to the church by taking the gospel out from Jerusalem across geographic, cultural, and ethnic barriers. Ask them to look at the plan for studying Acts in the table of contents in the *Study Guide*. Remind them that they have gathered to study today because those original disciples were faithful witnesses of Christ's story. Lead the class in prayer that this study

may encourage every member to be like those disciples and be faithful witnesses.

Guide Bible Study

3. Read Acts 1:1–5. Ask members to find Luke 24:36–53 and note that our text is a summary and continuation of the way Luke first told the story. Remind them that Luke was not an eyewitness to Christ's life, but in learning of it sent an account to Theophilus, a Roman (Luke 1:3). Note that Luke's written message is another of the ways the story moved to the Western, Gentile world.

4. Point out that Acts 1:3 says that Jesus provided "many convincing proofs" of his resurrection. Ask: *What level of proof do you think you would have needed to believe that Jesus was alive?*

5. Tell members that Jesus' promise of the baptism of the Holy Spirit was a key component in his provision for them to do the work he was equipping them to do. Read Acts 1:6–8. Note that Jesus promised that the Holy Spirit would empower the believers and provide all the resource they needed to be his witnesses. Ask: *In what ways are you aware that the Holy Spirit came on you when you became a follower of Christ?*

6. Ask: *What did Jesus mean when he said we would be his witnesses?* Encourage members to think about the difference between *doing* witnessing and *being* a witness. Remind them that in Matthew 28:18–20 Jesus said that the work of witnessing (*doing*) is to "make disciples" as we go about in life (*being*).

Encourage Application

7. Lead members to examine the small article, "Identifying Your Kingdom Assignment," in the *Study Guide*. Review the questions with the class, pausing after each one. Encourage participants to prayerfully consider a personal answer to each.

8. Close the session by reminding the class that because of the faithful witness of people for 2000 years, the story of Christ moved from

that one small gathering of disciples to us today. Lead the class in prayer that each member will be a faithful witness.

NOTES

1. Unless otherwise indicated, all Scripture quotations in lessons 1–3 and 9–11 are taken from the 1995 update of the New American Standard Bible®.

FOCAL TEXT
Acts 1:12–14; 2:1–18

BACKGROUND
Acts 1:12—2:36

MAIN IDEA
The Holy Spirit empowered
Jesus' followers to witness
to and minister for Jesus.

QUESTION TO EXPLORE
What actions are we
undertaking that require the
Spirit's power rather than
simply our own human efforts?

TEACHING AIM
To lead the class to evaluate
the extent to which they are
truly relying on the Spirit's
power in being Jesus' witnesses

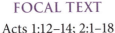

LESSON TWO
Rely On the Power of God's Spirit

BIBLE COMMENTS

Understanding the Context

The upper room at Jerusalem was a very busy place from the eve of the crucifixion of our Lord to the Day of Pentecost. Jesus himself had ordered his disciples to go and get the upper room ready for their celebration of the Passover. This was where they had the Last Supper, during which Jesus washed his disciples' feet. There he also made two startling predictions, that one of them would betray him and that Peter would deny him. There Jesus delivered his upper room discourse (John 14—16) and uttered his High Priestly prayer (John 17). It was in the upper room that the risen Lord appeared to his disciples on more than one occasion. Following the ascension of our Lord, it was in the upper room that the disciples elected Matthias to take the place of Judas Iscariot as an apostle (Acts 1:12–26). Finally, although Acts 2:1–2 does not identify it specifically, some Bible commentators believe it was in the upper room that the Holy Spirit descended on the disciples on the Day of Pentecost.

The risen Lord had ordered his disciples to remain in Jerusalem until they were "clothed with power from on high" (Luke 24:49), something "the Father had promised" (Acts 1:4). Luke was careful to let his readers know that the disciples obeyed this order. Thus he pointed out that after seeing the risen Lord ascend into heaven in full view of them all, the disciples returned to Jerusalem from Mount Olivet and, on arriving there, they "went up to the upper room where they were staying" (1:13). Luke gave us the detail that there were a total of about 120 disciples (Acts 1:15), made up of men and women, in the upper room when Peter addressed them, calling on them to elect someone to take the place of Judas Iscariot as an apostle (1:15). Note that while Jesus had twelve apostles, he had many other disciples. Luke emphasized that the disciples who were in the upper room were with one mind and that they were "continually devoting themselves to prayer" (1:14). It was presumably on this group of approximately one hundred and twenty disciples that the Holy Spirit descended on the Day of Pentecost.

Interpreting the Scriptures

The Coming of the Promised Power (2:1–3)

2:1. The coming of the promised power would be on the Day of Pentecost. "Pentecost" means *fiftieth* in Greek. The Feast of Pentecost was so called because it was celebrated on the fiftieth day from the first Sunday after Passover (see Leviticus 23:15–16). This means that in the year of our Lord's passion, the Feast of Pentecost was celebrated fifty days from the day when our Lord rose from the dead. On the Day of Pentecost, all the disciples were together in one place, presumably the upper room that he had talked about in Acts 1. They must have been praying, for that was what they were "continually devoting themselves to" (Acts 1:14). We do learn at the beginning of Peter's sermon that this took place in the morning (see 2:15).

2:2–3. These verses describe the experience that took place. The unusual noise the disciples heard could best be described as being similar to that of "a violent, rushing wind." They then saw a strange sight—what seemed like tongues of fire dividing themselves up into smaller parts and resting on each of them.

The Manifestation of the Received Power (2:4–36)

2:4. The disciples were all "filled with the Holy Spirit." Being filled with the Holy Spirit is not synonymous with being *baptized with the Holy Spirit*. Christians often debate on these phrases. Baptism with the Holy Spirit is synonymous with the indwelling of the Holy Spirit, and it usually takes place at the same point for any and every believer—at the moment of conversion. Every believer is indwelt by the Holy Spirit. Romans 8:9 states, "If anyone does not have the Spirit of Christ, he does not belong to Him." Since it is generally agreed by biblical scholars that the Spirit of Christ is synonymous with the Holy Spirit, the statement can be recast thus, *If anyone belongs to Christ, then that person has the Holy Spirit.*

Baptism with the Holy Spirit is to be differentiated from being "filled with the Spirit." A Christian who is filled with the Spirit is one who is controlled and empowered by the Holy Spirit. Such a person out of love has yielded completely to the Lord, is intent on obeying his commands implicitly, and therefore asks the Holy Spirit to direct his or her life on a continuous basis. Some wonder as to how often this can occur. It helps to note that, in talking of our Lord's disciples, while the Bible says that, "*All* were filled with the Holy Spirit" (Acts 2:4, italics added for emphasis) on the Day of Pentecost, a little later we are told, "After they had prayed, the place where they had gathered together was shaken, and they were *all* filled with the Holy Spirit and began to speak the word of God with boldness" (4:31, italics added for emphasis). All the apostles who had been filled with the Holy Spirit on the Day of Pentecost were once again filled with the Holy Spirit. This means that, unlike *baptism with the Holy Spirit,* which takes place only once for every Christian (usually at the moment of conversion), the filling of the Holy Spirit can, and should, occur more than once in a believer's life. Every believer is indwelt by the Holy Spirit (or *baptized with the Holy Spirit*), but not every believer is *filled with* (that is, controlled and empowered by) *the Holy Spirit.*

It's easy to be confused by the thought that the disciples in the upper room were "baptized by the Holy Spirit" on the Day of Pentecost (in fulfillment of Acts 1:5) and were also "filled with the Holy Spirit" on the same day and at the same time (Acts 2:4). However, this was because until then the Holy Spirit had not yet descended on the church, and this was the exception rather than the rule.

At no time should the Holy Spirit, the baptism of the Holy Spirit, or the filling with the Spirit be equated to any of the gifts of the Holy Spirit, such as speaking in tongues. There are believers who are filled with the Spirit who do not speak in tongues, and there are believers who speak in tongues who are not filled with (controlled and empowered by) the Holy Spirit. When the Bible commands believers to "be filled with the Spirit" (Ephesians 5:18), it is commanding believers to be controlled and empowered by the Holy Spirit, repeatedly, as an ongoing experience.

2:5–11. The disciples who had been "filled with the Holy Spirit . . . began to speak with other tongues" (2:4). Speaking with tongues is of two types. One type is *glossolalia,* which is best described as gibberish. The other type is speaking in an unknown language, in other words, in a language spoken by people, but one which that particular person had never learned. What the disciples experienced on the Day of Pentecost was this latter type. The Jews who had come to Jerusalem from different parts of the Roman Empire to celebrate the Feast of Pentecost heard the disciples who were from Galilee proclaiming in all of their different languages the wonderful deeds of God. Every part of the then-known world was represented.

2:12–13. Many of the people were amazed and wondered aloud what all of this could mean. They were seeing and hearing things they had never seen and heard before! However, some in the crowd, who had no better handle on the matter than the others, resorted to mocking the disciples, accusing them of being drunk.

2:14–15. Emboldened by the Holy Spirit, the apostles stood together, and Peter addressed the crowd. He delivered a moving message, beginning by mocking what some in the crowd were using to mock the disciples. He pointed out how ridiculous it was for anyone to suggest that they could all be drunk so early in the day, for it was only 9 a.m.

2:16. Peter authoritatively told them that what they were experiencing was a fulfillment of the prophecy of Joel.

2:17–18. Peter quoted directly from Joel 2, where the prophet Joel had prophesied that in the last days God would pour out his Spirit on all people—men and women, young and old, bondslaves and free people alike—and his Spirit would enable all these people to prophesy. Prophecy is of two kinds—*foretelling,* in which the one prophesying predicts what God will do in the future, and *forthtelling,* which is the proclamation of God's will for the present day. The latter is synonymous with preaching.

As the disciples utilized the power of the Holy Spirit and put that power into action, God's word did not go out in vain. The result was that people were convicted, those who were convicted believed, and those who believed were baptized into the body of Christ. About 3,000 people were saved on that glorious day (see Acts 2:37–41).

Focusing on the Meaning

How conscious are you of your need of the Holy Spirit's power? When is it easier for you to realize your need of the power of the Holy Spirit?

Is it when you know you are good at something or when you think you are simply mediocre at it? Is it when things are going smoothly or when things are not going so well? I am reminded of when the car I was driving was a clunker, going in and out of the repair shop. Whenever I used the car key to turn on the ignition, I remembered to pray, *Lord, p-l-e-a-s-e.* As the engine would start, I would say, *Thank you, Lord.* I am glad to say that the car I drive now is better than a clunker. The engine starts virtually every time I turn on the ignition. It dawned on me just the other day that it had been years since I prayed that my car engine would start. It had, therefore, been years since I said, *Thank you, Lord,* when my car engine started!

How many things do you think you can accomplish without the Holy Spirit's power? Jesus said, "Apart from Me, you can do nothing" (John 15:5). It is interesting to note that he did not say, "Apart from Me, you cannot do" *some things.* Neither did he say, "Apart from Me, you cannot do" *many things.* He said, "Apart from Me, you can do nothing." Whenever we quote Philippians 4:13, "I can do all things through Him who strengthens me," let us couple John 15:5 with it. We need to keep reminding ourselves that we cannot be Jesus' true witnesses without the empowerment of the Holy Spirit.

TEACHING PLANS

Teaching Plan—Varied Learning Activities

Connect with Life

1. Create a sense of anticipation among members by remaining silent for at least two minutes when it is time for you to begin the lesson. During this time of silence look at each person reflectively; do not answer any questions or make any announcement as to why you are silent. At the end of the time, ask, *How did the silence make you feel? What do you think I was doing by remaining silent?*

2. Tell participants that your purpose was to create anticipation in them by arousing curiosity about your intentions. Ask: *What are some familiar activities that do that by requiring us to wait for an extended period before they actually begin?* (Examples include preparations for a wedding or a big game, waiting on the birth of a child, uncertainty about medical test results, etc.)

3. Read Luke 24:45–49. Note that Jesus created anticipation with the disciples by telling them to go back to Jerusalem and to wait for God's Spirit to clothe them with "power from on high" (Luke 24:49). Tell members that one objective of this lesson is to gain a sense of expectancy that the same Holy Spirit will empower us to serve today. Lead the class in prayer for openness to the Spirit's leading.

Guide Bible Study

4. Lead members to read the lesson introduction in the *Study Guide,* which begins "Imagine a day without power." Invite one or two members to share briefly the inconveniences associated with being without electrical power for a time. Note the closing comment that addresses the availability of power for your spiritual life.

5. Write "The Power of Purposeful Waiting" on the board. Describe the difference between anticipation (optimistic expectancy) and anxiety (worried uncertainty). Ask members to comment on how they "waited" during your silence earlier. Ask: *What would you have done if instead of two minutes I had left the room for five or ten minutes?*

6. Enlist a member to read Acts 1:12–14. Ask: *What do you think is the key statement in this selection?* Note that the disciples went to their time of prayer expecting God to do something.

7. Ask: *To what degree do you believe our church regularly engages in praying expectantly?* Call attention to other factors involved in the disciples' prayer meeting (unity, confidence in the promise Jesus had given them).

8. Write "The Power of Promise and Provision" on the board. Remind the class that from Luke's account we assume the disciples had to wait at least ten days before Jesus' promise was fulfilled. Ask: *What do you think the disciples were expecting concerning what the Father was sending them?* (See Acts 1:4.)

9. Invite someone to read Acts 2:1–13. Ask members to circle words in the printed text in the *Study Guide* that describe the reactions of the "Jews from every nation under heaven" (Acts 2:5). Write these words on the board under the second heading: "amazement"; "great perplexity." Ask: *What was the source of these reactions by the people?* (hearing the gospel in their own language) Point out, too, the "mocking" on the part of others. Note that the purpose for the Spirit's coming, even with the remarkable *special effects,* was so that people could hear the gospel of Jesus Christ in their own language.

10. Write "The Power of the Spirit and You" on the board. Ask members to silently read Acts 2:14–18. Remind members that when Peter was last called on to testify of his love for Christ, he failed three times, just as Jesus had predicted. Ask: *What changed in Peter's life over the previous two months?* (experiences with the risen Jesus; coming of the Spirit)

11. Note in Acts 2:17–18 the repeated use of the statement: "I will pour forth of my Spirit." Remind the class that throughout his ministry Jesus had relied on the Spirit to be the empowering presence of the Father.

Encourage Application

12. Refer to and summarize "Implications and Actions" in the *Study Guide.* Ask members to reflect on their own awareness of the Spirit's empowering them for ministry. Encourage them to take a personal retreat from routine for even a couple of hours this week to wait expectantly for the Lord to reveal the ways he would empower them by *pouring out his Spirit* on them. Dismiss the session with prayer for courage and receptive hearts.

Teaching Plan—Lecture and Discussion

Connect with Life

1. Encourage members to think about a personal experience of waiting, such as the final days of a pregnancy or waiting for news from a doctor or a loan application. Invite one or two people to share briefly their feelings about the sense of anticipation or anxiety they felt. Note the difference between expecting good news (anticipation) and fearing bad news (anxiety).

2. Now invite a volunteer to describe the experience of finding that the battery in his or her car was dead. Talk briefly about the immediate emotional response, and then describe the rational actions that followed in order to get the car moving again. Ask: *In what ways does "having a dead battery" describe your spiritual life?*

3. Read Acts 1:4. Ask: *What do you imagine the disciples were thinking as they began their wait for the Father's promise?* Note that by commanding the disciples to wait for the promise, Jesus was giving them an opportunity to *re-charge their spiritual batteries* as they came together to pray and prepare for the mission he had given them. Lead in prayer.

Guide Bible Study

4. Guide members to read silently the first heading in the lesson in the *Study Guide*: "The Power of Purposeful Waiting." Enlist someone to read Acts 1:12–14. Ask the class to comment on the degree of motivation the disciples felt to pray as they returned from the Mount of Olives where they watched Jesus being taken into heaven.

5. Ask: *What things stand out in this passage about the disciples' attitudes as they returned to the upper room?* (They waited "with one mind," and they prayed constantly.) Ask a member to read Jeremiah 29:11–13. Ask: *What does the Jeremiah passage suggest to you about the purpose of the disciples' praying?*

6. Call attention to the following sentences in the *Study Guide*: "Waiting is not a *pause* in the process of God's work in our lives. Waiting is a *part* of the process of God's work in our lives." Encourage members to recognize that in each day we have many moments that could be devoted to "purposeful waiting" and seeking God's will for that day.

7. Have someone read Acts 2:1–13 while participants listen for what happened. Note that we often focus on the spectacular way the Holy Spirit came that day, but that we see in this passage the emphasis that the gospel was proclaimed so all the people could understand it in their own languages. Ask: *What does this tell us about the role and purpose of the Holy Spirit?*

8. Have someone read Acts 2:14–18. Remind the class about Peter's experience as he betrayed Jesus. Ask: *What happened to Peter in the fifty days since those betrayals?* Encourage members to look at 2:17–18. Ask: *What did the prophet say would be the result of God pouring out his Spirit?*

Encourage Application

9. Ask members to close their eyes and reflect silently on their commitment to the truth of the following statements:
   - I believe that the Holy Spirit is God's gift to every believer, including me.
   - I believe that the Holy Spirit gave the disciples a unique way to tell others the story of Jesus, and that the Holy Spirit will also give me what I need to tell others about Jesus.
   - I believe that there are people around me who need to know Jesus' story and trust him as Savior.

10. Close by asking members to do *purposeful praying* this week as they reflect on those three statements.

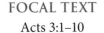

LESSON THREE

Engage in Holistic Witness for Jesus

BIBLE COMMENTS

Understanding the Context

The events of the Day of Pentecost ushered in a new day in the history of the church. The Holy Spirit descended on all the disciples present that day, and at the end of Peter's sermon about 3,000 people came to know the Lord. These new believers were baptized into the fellowship of the church. The body of believers thus got a double shot in the arm. Luke used four main aspects to describe the activities of this early church. He said that the disciples "were continually devoting themselves to the apostle's teaching and to fellowship, to the breaking of bread and to prayer" (Acts 2:42).

The believers were *together,* meaning that they were united in spirit and in fellowship. A practical demonstration of this unity was that they enjoyed the community of goods, voluntarily pooling their resources together, so that none of them lacked anything, since sharing was done on the basis of need. They tirelessly praised God as they worshiped him in the temple, broke bread from house to house, and ate together gladly and sincerely (see Acts 2:44–47).

The unbelieving community was gripped by a sense of awe as the apostles performed "many wonders and signs" (2:43). Evidently, these signs and wonders were similar to the mighty works that Jesus had performed, for Peter would refer to Jesus' mighty works as "miracles and wonders and signs" (2:22).

Luke then proceeded to give his readers an example of how the Holy Spirit was using the apostles in performing these signs and wonders. He described how Peter healed the lame man "at the gate of the temple which is called Beautiful" (3:2).

Interpreting the Scriptures

Peter and John Encounter the Lame Man (3:1–2)

3:1. Peter and John, two of Jesus' apostles, were on their way doing what was customary to them. They were going into the temple at 3 p.m. This was the time of the afternoon sacrifice, and it was accompanied by prayer for the congregation.

3:2. They saw a lame man who was being carried by his loved ones to one of the gates of the temple, the Gate Beautiful. This was something they did faithfully, carrying him daily and putting him down by the gate so that he could beg alms of the worshipers who were entering the temple. The case looked hopeless, and there was no end in sight, save the death of the lame man. The man had been lame from his mother's womb and was now more than forty years old (see 4:22).

Lameness was viewed seriously in the Old Testament. It was one of the conditions (defects) that barred anyone, even a descendant of Aaron, from performing the priestly duties in the temple (see Leviticus 21:17–23).

The Lame Man Asks for Alms (3:3)

The lame man saw Peter and John about to enter the temple, and he asked them for alms. In the lame man's mind, this was the only way in which anyone could help him.

Peter and John Heal the Lame Man (3:4–10)

3:4–5. Peter and John looked intently at the lame man, and Peter said to him, "Look at us!" That must have raised the man's hope. He must have thought that they were about to give him a huge amount of money. He looked expectantly at them.

3:6. If Peter's words, "Look at us," raised the lame man's hopes, Peter's next few words must have dashed any hope he had, for Peter said, "I do not possess silver and gold." The lame man must have felt like saying, *Then what made you ask me to look at you?* But Peter's next few words would be life-changing words for this man who had never known what it was like to walk. Peter continued by saying, "But what I do have I give to you: In the name of Jesus Christ the Nazarene—walk!"

3:7. This was a man who had never taken a step in his life, and so Peter grabbed him by the right hand and lifted him up. Healing was instantaneous: "Immediately his feet and his ankles were strengthened."

3:8. The healing was also dramatic. The man who had been lame stood upright and began to walk. As he entered the temple with Peter and John, he was ecstatic, "walking and leaping and praising God."

Peter and John Use the Healing as an Opportunity to Share the Gospel (3:9–10)

The people who were in the temple could not help but notice this man walking and praising God. They were struck with wonder and amazement, for they recognized this man as the man who had been lame all of his life and who used to sit at the Beautiful Gate of the temple begging alms.

When the people saw this man who had been lame all of his life walking with Peter and John and clinging to them, they all ran towards them. They happened to be in the part of the temple that was called "the portico of Solomon" (Acts 3:11). The portico of Solomon was close to the court of the Gentiles.

Peter and John could tell that the people were now in danger of deifying them, and so Peter seized this opportunity to preach to the people (3:12). In his sermon, Peter pointed out that the people were focusing their attention on them as though their own power or piety had enabled the man to walk. On the contrary, he said, it was the name of Jesus, through faith in his name, that had healed the man (see 3:16). Peter called on them to repent and return to the Lord so that their sins might be "wiped away" (3:19).

Holistic Witnessing

Peter and John engaged in holistic witnessing for Jesus. Holistic witnessing is witnessing that aims at having an effect on the whole person, not just on getting the person saved. Peter and John encountered the lame man, and they realized the need to take care of the man's physical need before tackling his spiritual problem. Their healing the man would open the door to their preaching the gospel not only to the man but also to the crowd who would end up gathering around them.

Peter and John were following Jesus' example. Matthew 15:29–39 gives us a case in point. The passage talks of how great multitudes came to Jesus, "bringing with them those who were lame, crippled, blind, dumb, and many others, and they laid them down at His feet, and He healed them" (Matthew 15:30). The people "glorified the God of Israel" (Matt. 15:31), and Jesus preached the gospel to them. Jesus would later express his concern for the people's need for food, as he told his disciples, "I feel compassion for the multitude, because they have been with Me now three days and have nothing to eat" (Matt. 15:32). He proceeded to perform a miracle, feeding the thousands of people who were there. Jesus healed the people, preached to them, and fed them. This was a holistic presentation of the gospel.

Jesus' holistic presentation of the gospel was in step with his earthly mission. In the synagogue in Nazareth where he had grown up, Jesus declared that he was the fulfillment of Isaiah's prophecy which basically talked about meeting the needs of the people and proclaiming the gospel to them (see Luke 4:18–19; Isaiah 61:1–2). Not surprisingly, therefore, when John the Baptist who was imprisoned by Herod Antipas sent two of his disciples to Jesus, Jesus would give them the following answer, "Go and report to John what you have seen and heard: the BLIND RECEIVE SIGHT, the lame walk, the lepers are cleansed, and the deaf hear, the dead are raised up, the POOR HAVE THE GOSPEL PREACHED TO THEM" (Luke 7:22). He was doing exactly what the Messiah was supposed to do and giving us an example in the process.

Focusing on the Meaning

Jesus engaged in the holistic preaching of the gospel, and so did Peter and John and the other apostles. One has to be intentional in a holistic preaching of the gospel. Suppose you come by an unbeliever who is half-naked, hungry, and looking as if he has not had a bath in five days. As you talk to him, he explains that he takes a bath daily, but that he is unable to afford soap. You have the resources to help this man. How would you minister to him?

One school of thought would be to present the gospel to this man without wasting any time. Since the soul is more important than the body, meeting his spiritual need is far more important than meeting his physical needs. Know that his physical needs would somehow be satisfied.

Another school of thought would be to say that in order to show this man that you care you ought to give him food to eat, soap for him to bathe with, and clothes to wear, thus letting him know that you do care for his total well-being, and then present the gospel to him. You would actually have his undivided attention this way, and so get him to listen to the gospel message. The former school of thought is only half right, while the latter school of thought is totally right. Of course, a totally wrong school of thought is to say that all you need to care about are the physical needs of the man.

Most churches have difficulty striking a good balance here. Many churches that are strongly evangelistic are weak in ministry to the needy. On the other hand, many churches that are strong in ministry to the needy are weak in evangelism. We need to realize that to emphasize one and neglect the other is to fail to engage in the holistic preaching of the gospel.

TEACHING PLANS

Teaching Plan—Varied Learning Activities

Connect with Life

1. Pre-arrange with a person experienced in providing care for the elderly or other long-term disability needs to visit your class. Ask the caregiver to discuss the kinds of needs faced by the patient (medical, feeding, sanitary, and/or emotional issues). Encourage the provider to be as specific as possible.

2. Begin by introducing the guest and telling members that providing care for aging and severely disabled people is among the most recognizable of the compassionate ministries in church life. Ask the guest to describe his or her role as a caregiver, highlighting the list of physical and emotional needs that need to be addressed.

3. Tell members that the purpose of the guest's visit is to highlight one kind of need that is present in many different forms in every community, and that it can serve to help believers become increasingly sensitive to a variety of practical needs among people we encounter daily.

Guide Bible Study

4. Enlist someone to read Acts 3:1–5. Ask members to focus on verse 2 and imagine the scene from the perspective of three characters: the lame man; the people who carried him to the temple; and those who saw and heard him begging for alms. Ask: *Where are you in this scene today? Are you the person with a need, a helper, or one of the observers?*

5. Note that we often pass people who are in need—financial, emotional, spiritual—and, because we are accustomed to seeing them, we may keep going without ever considering the need in their lives.

6. Ask members to look at verse 3. Encourage discussion about whether Peter and John would have passed him by if the man had not cried out for alms. Emphasize that the important part of that encounter is that the apostles stopped to help, called for the man's attention, and became true care-givers.

7. Read Acts 3:6–10. Ask members to think about a personal experience when a burden was lifted from their shoulders. Ask: *How would you describe this man's reaction to discovering that his "feet and ankles became strong"?* Remind the class that in Acts 2:43 Luke stated that a sense of awe had developed among the people because "many wonders and signs were taking place through the apostles."

8. Ask: *What is significant about the method Peter used to help the man?* Consider that the man's personal vision was limited: he

hoped only for alms. Yet Peter offered more. He gave him physical healing, and with it he introduced him to Jesus Christ of Nazareth.

9. Guide participants to discuss their reaction if they had been physically present to see the man "walking and leaping and praising God" (3:8). Ask: *Do you think you are likely to be more impressed by a testimony of physical healing or by a story about a person who has come to Christ from a rough, sin-filled life? Why?*

Encourage Application

10. Note that in the accounts that follow, Peter used the opportunity of the gathered crowd to proclaim at great personal risk (see Acts 4:3) that Jesus is the Christ. Ask: *What lesson does Peter's response suggest about our efforts at meeting others' needs?*

11. Encourage members to reflect on the guest's presentation of needs of people who are confined by age and/or disease. Ask: *What are some needs we should see in other people?* Encourage them to think about co-workers and neighbors and to consider economic, family, health, and especially spiritual issues.

12. Close by urging members to prayerfully consider identifying at least one person with these needs, and to begin praying for awareness of their needs and the courage to reach out to meet them.

Teaching Plan—Lecture and Questions

Connect with Life

1. Tell the following story:

> Jesse was a sixty-seven-year old man with cerebral palsy who loved the Lord and his church. He lived by himself in a government apartment and rode to church on the church van. Although the apartment complex provided assistance because of his disability, Jesse's personal hygiene was not good. He was bathed each Tuesday by an aide, but

by Sunday morning he arrived at church dirty, in smelly clothes. Jesse could not speak clearly and his pronounced limp and withered arms meant that he could not get around very well, but he always had a smile on his face.

2. Ask: *If Jesse attended our church, how could our class demonstrate that God loves him?*

Guide Bible Study

3. Invite someone to read Acts 3:1–5. Ask: *In what ways can you compare Jesse's situation with the beggar who was carried to the temple gate each day?* Note that the lame man's response when he saw Peter and John was to ask for money. Enlist a participant to read John 5:1–8. Invite discussion about the question Jesus asked, and encourage members to think about the sense of helplessness people such as the man in the John story and the lame man at the temple may have felt. Ask: *Do you think the lame man in the temple expected anything more than money from those who passed by?*

4. Have someone read Acts 3:4–5. Tell the class that when both Peter and John looked at the man, they were telling him that he was important and that he deserved their attention. Ask: *How do you think this made the lame man feel? How do you think this was different from the probable response of most others who walked by him?*

5. Enlist someone to read Acts 3:6–10. Briefly describe the nature of authority that Peter invoked by offering healing in the name of Jesus Christ of Nazareth. Explain these verses further using information in the *Study Guide* and in "Bible Comments" in this *Teaching Guide.*

6. Call attention to the lesson title, "Engage in Holistic Witness." Remind them that Peter's gift was far greater than physical healing, but that because the man's physical challenge had been the dominant factor in his entire life, healing became the opportunity to share a verbal witness of Christ.

Encourage Application

7. Remind members that in our culture, a request for financial assistance is often the primary way people reach out to us, and that making a donation can make us feel we have *done our part.* Tell them that the story of Jesse is true, and that a men's Bible study class and a women's Bible study class began working together to help him. Each Sunday someone from the men's class would give Jesse a bath, and each week someone from the women's class would wash his clothes and linens.

8. Ask: *Who is like Jesse in our church or in our community?* Remind members that loving our neighbors includes caring for physical, emotional, and spiritual needs, and that the same Holy Spirit who empowered Peter to preach before thousands gave him strength to love the lame man.

9. Challenge members to identify at least one person or group who is like the lame man or like Jesse, and to think about specific ways the class could minister in the name of Jesus. Close the session in prayer.

FOCAL TEXT

Acts 4:5–31

BACKGROUND

Acts 4

MAIN IDEA

The disciples prayed for and exercised boldness in serving as Jesus' witnesses.

QUESTION TO EXPLORE

How can we exercise greater boldness in serving as Jesus' witnesses?

TEACHING AIM

To lead participants to decide on ways they will exercise greater boldness in serving as Jesus' witnesses

LESSON FOUR

Pray for Boldness in Being Jesus' Witness

BIBLE COMMENTS

Understanding the Context

Three o'clock in the afternoon, and everything was as usual for one man. He could not walk, and so his friends carried him to the gate called "Beautiful," where he planned to spend his day asking for money. Day after day he sat and begged; and this was another one of those days. But this was to be no ordinary day for him, for the people who knew him, or for Peter and John.

The man appealed to Peter and John for a contribution as they approached. They had no money, but they did have a greater gift to give. Peter commanded him in the name of Jesus to "stand up and walk" (Acts 3:6; see 3:1–10, lesson 3).[1] The man did. We can imagine the joy he felt. No one had to carry him anymore. He could walk, or even run, to where he wanted to go—all because of Jesus. Peter and John knew that they were in the mission and purpose of Jesus, and they acted.

Word quickly spread about a man made well. A crowd gathered. Peter stood before the crowd and boldly proclaimed Jesus, the one the people previously rejected and helped to crucify, but who was now raised from the dead (3:15–16). Believing that Peter and John were leading the people astray because they preached that in Jesus was the resurrection of the dead (4:1–2), the Sadducees had them arrested. Sadducees did not believe in a resurrection. They viewed only the first five books of the Old Testament as being Scripture, which to them had no reference to a resurrection or an afterlife. Pharisees, who were laity and not priests, did believe in a resurrection.

The two apostles proclaiming the resurrection of Jesus as an accomplished fact threatened the status and authority of the Sadducees. The healing of the man, however, meant the exercise of some kind of power that they could not deny before the people, and so the Sadducees had to deal with the two apostles.

Interpreting the Scriptures

The Opposing Powers (4:5–8)

4:5–6. Real life always has dramatic narrative, which was especially true of Jesus' followers as they participated in the new frontier of his kingdom rule. The setting of this narrative begins with a gathering of the powerful on one side and the seemingly powerless on the other. The powerful side was the Sanhedrin, the official ruling body of the Jews. Composed of seventy members, they primarily decided matters of religious law with civil law matters belonging to the occupying Romans.

To gather the religious leaders against two prisoners indicates how seriously they considered the threat against the religious establishment. By means of the miracle, they introduced the reality of the resurrection of Jesus and his kingdom rule, a kingdom rule in contrast to the rule of the temple and religious powers.

4:7–8. The rulers questioned "by what power or by what name" Peter and John had healed the man, which was to ask about the source of their authority and power. Peter, "filled with the Holy Spirit" (4:8), was ready to answer them. To be "filled" meant they had a new experience with the Spirit, as before at Pentecost, that prepared them and equipped them for the task at hand.

Boldness to Answer the Authorities (4:9–12)

4:9. The best situation for the defense is to be asked to defend a *good* deed, of course, not a bad one. By referring to the man now well, Peter really put the burden of examination back on the religious leaders. How were they to explain that the man who could not walk now walked? They could not, and so Peter explained it to them.

4:10. Peter and John acted in the "name" of Jesus. Acting in the "name" was to act in the nature, purpose, authority, and power of Jesus. Only Jesus through the Holy Spirit could equip Peter and John to do what they did. It would be tough to deny the healed man and the resurrection at the same time since it was by the resurrected Lord that the man was able to walk.

4:11–12. Peter was bold about criticizing the rulers. He referred to them as "builders" (4:11) by quoting from Psalm 118:22. As used here, interpreters make various applications of the "stone" reference: the stone that holds the walls together; the keystone in an arch that holds the structure together; a foundation stone; and a stone that guides the shaping of the rest of the building. Peter told the council that they the "builders" rejected the very stone necessary for them to build the building of Israel. Now the Sanhedrin was on trial.

The Accused Are Bold (4:13)

This verse is an appropriate focus for this lesson on boldness. Peter and John acted out their belief in an intimidating and threatening situation. The fountainhead of boldness lies in what one believes and the degree of commitment to that belief as compared with everything else. Their knowledge of why and what they were doing "amazed" the council. To say they were "uneducated and ordinary" meant that they were not trained by the rabbis or in any formal educational sense. Of course, spending up to three years with Jesus in both listening to him and seeing him in action was the best formal education possible.

The Authorities in a Quandary (4:14–17)

4:14–15. The rulers found themselves in a dilemma. They wanted to blunt the impact of the influential witness of Peter and John to the resurrected Christ, but it proved difficult to bring stiff charges and penalties against them in light of the good thing done for a human being. Indeed, how could they place themselves in opposition to the good? They dismissed the prisoners until they found a solution.

4:16–17. Their best solution under the circumstances was to silence Peter and John. Silencing voices is the way the powerful subdue those who challenge them. The rulers had the option of listening to Peter and John to see whether what they said was true. They refused although the healed man was there as evidence.

A Bold Response (4:18–20)

The order came from the authoritative body of the Jews: don't say anything in the "name of Jesus" (4:18) again. The defendants challenged the council to answer for themselves whether it was best to listen to God or to them. However, Peter and John stated boldly what they would do; they would not be silent for they must "keep speaking about what they have seen and heard."

An Effective Defense and Witness (4:21–23)

4:21. The religious authorities tried to silence and play down the whole healing event and subsequent witness to Christ in order to protect their honor and power. But the "people" continued to praise "God for what happened." The council released the apostles, "threatening them again," again indicating that they were to be silent about Jesus.

4:22–23. The man who had been healed was an adult, "more than forty years old" (4:22), and it was remarkable that a person that much into adulthood could be healed. Because of the praise and excitement of the people over the event, the authorities preferred not to go against Peter and John by assigning further punishment.

The Church Celebrates (4:23–26)

4:23. Once Peter and John were freed, they went directly to "their friends" (4:23), to the church. Peter and John's boldness in the resurrected Jesus received additional support from a praying and worshiping church.

4:24–26. The church responded by worshiping God. They turned to the Psalms to help them express their praise and prayer. The first reference celebrates that God, "who made the heaven and the earth, the sea, and everything in them" (Psalm 146:6), delivers those under threats and oppression. Then they expressed Psalm 2:1–2. This psalm refers to the nations that "conspire" (Ps. 2:1) and "kings of the earth" who are against God's "anointed" (Ps. 2:2). "Anointed" refers to God's specially anointed one who is the Messiah, the King. "Gentiles" in the Acts text (Acts 4:25) is to be understood not as an ethnic identity but as a reference to those who are not God's people. In this case, the authorities who crucified Jesus and persecuted the church were the "Gentiles."

The Celebration Continues (4:27–28)

The church was specific about those who crucified Jesus. Both Herod and Pontius Pilate were responsible, corresponding to the kings and rulers in Psalm 2:2, who set themselves against the anointed. They also were the "Gentiles." But the "peoples of Israel" conspired with the Gentiles to bring about the crucifixion of Jesus. Those who were not God's people and those who were called to be God's people and thus respond to Jesus the Messiah joined forces against God's "holy servant Jesus."

Onward with Boldness (4:29–31)

The church, though, saw victory in the experience of Peter and John and future victory. What was needed was bold commitment and witness on their part. So they prayed for boldness to "speak your word" (Acts 4:29)—that is, to live and to give witness to Christ. If they did so, they knew God would support them with "signs and wonders" through the "name" of "Jesus" (4:30). Again they had the experience of being "filled with the Holy Spirit," enabling them to speak "with boldness" (4:31) in the tasks given them.

Focusing on the Meaning

The response of Peter and John inspired and inspires persecuted and ostracized Christians across the centuries to stand against authority in the name of Jesus. With the Baptist belief in the priesthood of believers, soul competency, and soul freedom, their words have been something of the watchword response when threatening authorities challenge that soul competency and soul freedom.

As the account unfolds in today's lesson, it is evident that prayer, boldness, and action are together. The church prays for boldness, and then they act on that for which they prayed. This suggests that to pray for boldness and then wait to act on that boldness is not the right approach.

We pray for boldness and then act. The boldness becomes a reality in the action itself. Of course, as we pray and trust, we experience calmness and encouragement. Nonetheless, we may experience anxiety or fear when the call for boldness comes.

Our boldness does not arise strictly from ourselves. Jesus' resurrection is a prominent feature in our focal text. We serve a living Jesus who is with us through the Holy Spirit. Our boldness also will be within the relationship of the living Christ himself. Also prominent in this Scripture passage is the presence of Jesus' church. Jesus called us into being as his church so we can encourage and support one another and act together. The church is called to worship and pray together to be on bold mission for Christ.

TEACHING PLANS

Teaching Plan—Varied Learning Activities

Connect with Life

1. Begin the study session by calling on a member to lead in prayer for your time together. Check with the learner beforehand to make sure he or she feels comfortable.

2. Using a whiteboard or a flip chart, lead learners in listing people they would consider *bold*. (The discipline or field to which the person is related does not matter.) Do not allow learners to explain their answers at this time. In fact, give learners the following instructions for brainstorming:
    - Don't explain why you mentioned a particular person's name just yet.
    - Don't criticize the offering of a particular person's name just yet.

3. Enlist a volunteer to serve as a scribe to record names on the list. After at least ten names have been recorded, lead in discussion about why the individuals on the list should or should not be considered *bold.*

4. Share with learners that today we're going to witness one of the greatest examples of true *boldness* ever known.

Guide Bible Study

5. Refer to the *Study Guide* and the "Bible Comments" section in this *Teaching Guide* to understand, clarify, and explain biblical material throughout the lesson.

6. Invite someone to recall the events in the Scripture for lesson three, on Acts 3:1–10. Summarize briefly Acts 3:11—4:4.

7. Then enlist a volunteer to read Acts 4:5–12. Enlist another volunteer to summarize the encounter of Peter and John with the rulers and elders. Make clarifications or fill in the gaps to the volunteer's summary as necessary. Lead the class in a guided discussion focusing on these questions: *What do these verses teach us about God? What do these verses teach us about people? What do these verses teach us about life in general?*

8. Call for a volunteer to read Acts 4:13–22. Enlist another volunteer to share their understanding of "boldness" as demonstrated by Peter and John. Summarize the passage and explain why the expression "more than forty years old" (4:22) was deemed important in the context.

9. Lead learners in a guided discussion focusing on the following questions: *What is the meaning of the phrase "unschooled, ordinary men" (NIV84)? What is the significance of Peter and John being described this way? What is the life lesson you glean from this passage?*

10. Have a volunteer read Acts 4:23–31. Summarize the passage. Emphasize the importance of having a local church community.

11. Lead learners in a guided discussion focusing on these questions: *What does this passage teach you about God? What does this passage teach you about people? What does this passage teach you about life in general?*

Encourage Application

12. Direct learners to take out their cell phones. If they don't have them, then ask them to take out their imaginary cell phones. Ask them to look at their phones (allow for at least sixty seconds). Instruct them to imagine that they just received a text from the Apostle Peter. The text tells them what they should do during the next seven days to be a bold witness for Jesus. Direct them to record the message on a sheet of paper.

13. End the session by asking the same member who opened the class with prayer to close the class by praying that each learner will respond to the text about Peter faithfully.

Teaching Plan—Lecture and Questions

Connect with Life

1. Use this lesson outline (taken from the *Study Guide*):

Pray for Boldness in Being Jesus' Witness (Acts 4:5–31)
The disciples prayed for and exercised boldness in serving as Jesus' witnesses.

I. Speaking Before the High Court (4:5–15):

II. Ordinary Men With Boldness (4:13–22):

III. Believers Pray for Continued Boldness (4:23–31):

The outline is available on a lesson handout in "Teaching Resource Items" for this study at www.baptistwaypress.org. Prior to class beginning, place a copy of the lesson handout in the chair of each learner. If you use the handout, learners should be able to follow along more attentively with the lesson as they fill in blanks while you teach and interact with them.

2. Begin class by asking a member to pray for your time together. Check with the learner beforehand to make sure he or she feels comfortable praying in pubic.

3. Introduce the lesson by using the illustration, "Never Lose to Fear," as follows:

    The story is told of a young man who was participating in a martial arts tournament. He had progressed nicely up to the championship match of the tournament when he was faced with his toughest opponent. This was troubling because his opponent was taller, stronger, faster, and maybe even better than he was.

    The match included three three-minute rounds. By the end of the second round, the young man was beaten, battered, and bruised. During the intermission between the second and final round, the young man lay face down on the mat with an injured leg and broken spirit. He started to cry and told his coach he did not want to fight anymore. He wanted to give up. His coached asked him why he wanted to give up. The young man shouted, "I'm afraid!" The coach responded, "It's all right to lose to an opponent, but you must never lose to fear!" It turns out that his biggest opponent wasn't the other fighter. His biggest opponent was fear.

    For Christians, the biggest obstacle to being faithful witnesses for Christ many times is not Satan or the world. But it is the fear inside of us.

4. Review the Question to Explore from the *Study Guide*. Share with the class that you will ask this question throughout the lesson.

Guide Bible Study

5. Refer to the *Study Guide* and the "Bible Comments" section in this *Teaching Guide* to understand, clarify, and explain biblical material throughout the lesson.

6. Recall the events in the Scripture for lesson three, on Acts 3:1–10. Summarize briefly Acts 3:11—4:4.

7. Enlist a volunteer to read Acts 4:5–12. Direct learners' attention to the lesson handout that focuses on "Speaking Before the High Court." Encourage learners to use the space below the subject headings to freely record their thoughts as the Lord brings them to mind.

8. Explain the encounter in Acts 4:5–12. Clarify the intensity and danger of the conflict Peter and John had with the authorities. Discuss why Peter and John were described as being *bold*.

9. Ask the Question to Explore again. Then instruct learners to add *Practice Boldness* to their lesson handout.

10. Enlist a volunteer to read Acts 4:13–22. Direct learners' attention to the lesson handout that focuses on "Ordinary Men with Boldness." Explain the meaning of "boldness" and suggest examples of "boldness" from the Book of Acts and from the history of the church. Ask question two from the Questions section of the *Study Guide*.

11. Ask the Question to Explore. Then instruct learners to add *Persist in Boldness* to their lesson handout.

12. Enlist a volunteer to read Acts 4:23–31. Direct learners' attention to the lesson handout that focuses on "Believers Pray for Continued Boldness." Explain why the believers prayed for "boldness," and discuss the results of their prayer.

13. Ask the Question to Explore again. Then instruct learners to add *Pray for Boldness* to their lesson handout.

Encourage Application

14. Ask learners to ponder what has been discussed during the lesson. Instruct learners to write in the space at the bottom of the lesson handout what they will do this week to exercise "boldness" as a witness for Christ.

15. Preview the Study Aim for the next lesson by referring to the *Study Guide.*

16. End class by asking the same member who opened the class with prayer to close the class with prayer.

N O T E S ───

1. Unless otherwise indicated, all Scripture quotations in lesson 4–6 and 12–13 are from the New Revised Standard Version Bible.

FOCAL TEXT

Acts 6:1–7; 11:27–30

BACKGROUND

Acts 6:1–15; 8:1; 11:27–30; 12:25

MAIN IDEA

The early church extended help to people in need, near and far.

QUESTION TO EXPLORE

How does ministry to human need relate to being Jesus' witnesses?

TEACHING AIM

To lead participants to describe how the churches at Jerusalem and Antioch ministered to human need and plan to engage in at least one action that will extend their Christian witness by ministering to human need

LESSON FIVE
Minister to Human Need

BIBLE COMMENTS

Understanding the Context

Unintentionally perhaps, we sometimes seem to refer to a person as composed of a physical self and a spiritual self as if a human is two separate parts. If we think this way, we are reflecting the influence of Greek thought on our concept of person. The Bible will sometimes refer to a person in terms of body, heart, spirit, or soul, but more in the sense of looking at the whole person from one of these particular standpoints. Greek thought, influenced strongly by the thought of Plato, viewed a person as *having* a soul, while the biblical view would be expressed more closely by saying a person *is* a soul. In resurrection, for example, the whole person, although transformed into resurrected body (see 1 Corinthians 15), is raised. We are not lost; we are saved. Jesus saves the whole person.

The context of this text about ministering to the needs of others is Jesus. Luke is the author of both Luke and Acts. In the Gospel of Luke, Jesus' concern began with the marginalized, the needy, those usually rejected or un-empowered. Even Jesus' parables make the principal figure to be the person in need. For example, in the parable of the Good Samaritan (Luke 10:30–37), the beaten, unidentified person by the road, a person in great need, is helped by the Samaritan who himself would be rejected by many in Jewish society. The prodigal son (Luke 15:11–32) in his utterly destitute state is one main focus of attention in the parable of the Prodigal Son. A description that characterizes Jesus is that "he went about doing good" (Acts 10:38). Jesus loves the whole person as a person is, and we are commissioned to minister to the needs of the whole person as we follow the path of Jesus.

Interpreting the Scriptures

A Need Made Known (6:1)

The young Christian community readily shared its resources with those in need. In this case, the widows were the focus. Widows often were the most destitute in society, because wealth, little or much, came by way of the husband's abilities and resources. Most families were unable to store much should something happen to the husband, and so the widow, and likewise the orphan, had to depend on others. Judaism emphasized taking care of the widows, and so some charity system was usually in place. The early church had its charity system for those of its community, which at this time had become a large community.

"Hellenists" are explained by some interpreters as Greek-speaking Jews, and "Hebrews" as Hebrew-speaking Jews. Others say the Hellenists were simply Jews who had immigrated to Palestine after having grown up in other cultures while maintaining their Jewish heritage.

Perhaps the majority "Hebrews," who were more local in their origin, unconsciously favored the distribution of food to other "Hebrews." Or perhaps there was some prejudice against those immigrant Jews who did not have the Hebrews' long-standing local history. In any case, the "Hellenists" complained that their widows did not receive enough attention in the "daily distribution of food."

The Leaders Act (6:2–3)

6:2. The leaders were the "twelve," a title that designated the apostles, Jesus' chosen disciples. Of course, Judas, who betrayed Jesus, was not with them, but still there were twelve. Matthias had been chosen to take Judas's place (Acts 1:26), and although Matthias's name does not appear again in Acts or elsewhere, evidently he assumed his responsibilities along with the original eleven. The Twelve wisely "called together the whole community" to be involved in the complaint's solution.

Acts 2:42 indicates that the community depended on the apostles for teaching and leadership in "fellowship," "breaking of bread" (a reference to the Lord's Supper as well), and "prayers." So, it is understandable that they could not drop those responsibilities in order to "wait on tables." Charity work was a serious matter in Jewish life, requiring organization, time, and effort, and so the Twelve were not dismissing this matter as trivial. The fact that they called together the whole community to deal with the matter indicates the matter was important.

A Solution Found (6:3–4)

The whole matter might have disintegrated into a disruptive community squabble, which would have gone directly against the "breaking of bread" (2:42) in observance of the Lord's Supper. In light of Jesus' giving himself, it was ludicrous to squabble over the bread (resources) distributed to the widows.

The Twelve indicated that they needed to devote themselves "to prayer and to serving the word." Whatever the church does, including helping those in need, it should have a theological or belief base for its ministry. That is the reason those to be appointed needed to be "full of the Spirit" (6:3) and the reason the disciples needed to give attention to their teaching, preaching, and praying responsibilities. Without anchoring actions in Christ, his life, and his teachings, matters become shaped by power struggles and selfishness even in the church. The Twelve wanted to keep the Word, Jesus, central in their ministry.

The Community Pulls Together (6:5–7)

6:5. The manner in which the complaint was handled indicates that no effort was afoot to use authority to control the resources of the community. The church was on board with the Twelve's leadership, accepting readily the new organizational structure to distribute resources.

Note that meeting human need under the leadership of the Spirit was the organizational principle at this moment. Churches certainly need to seek the Holy Spirit's guidance as they anticipate meeting the human needs that put themselves in their paths.

Interestingly, those selected to serve the daily distribution of food, which likely involved financial management as well, apparently were Hellenists since they had Greek names. One was a proselyte, Nicolaus, a Gentile who adopted the Jewish faith. Ultimately turning the matter over to those who lodged the complaint was an act of wise administration. In this event, everyone was involved in meeting the church's needs and ministry.

Those chosen were spiritually prepared for the task. Observe that Stephen and Philip are the first two named. Stephen would help to distribute resources, and he would do more. His story occupies half of Acts 6 and all of Acts 7. He was a passionate witness for Christ, angering a group so much that, evidently under the encouragement of one named Saul, they became a mob and stoned Stephen to death (7:54—8:1). As far as we know, Stephen was the first Christian martyr.

Philip became a dynamic witness for Jesus as well. He shared the gospel as he went, and many Samaritans became followers of Jesus (8:4–8). Also, Philip shared with an Ethiopian eunuch, and he became a disciple of Christ (8:27–39). According to tradition, the Ethiopian took the gospel to Africa when he returned home. Whenever the church organizes to meet human need under the leadership and preparation of the Spirit, the church certainly will be led into surprising opportunities to witness for Jesus.

6:6–7. The church, by laying on of hands, ordained those selected for the ministry. Placing hands on them conferred no special powers. Rather it was an act of blessing and support by the church. While not deacons in a later New Testament sense, these do serve as something of a prototype of deacon service that came later in church development.

Ordination indicates the seriousness of the matter of distributing resources to meet needs. Helping others is no trivial matter. Service to meet human need, although it may seem small in relation to far-reaching tasks, is of great significance to Christ.

Cooperative Effort to Serve Others' Needs (11:27–30)

11:27. Two major churches in the Christian movement existed at this time: the church at Jerusalem and the church at Antioch. The church at Antioch (see Acts 13) gave its attention more and more to a mission focused on Gentiles, while the church at Jerusalem focused on Jews and proselytes. Both churches worked to make a vital relationship with each other.

11:28. The Pharisees believed that the prophetic role for Israel belonged to the past and that the rabbis generally were the voice of God's message to Israel. Jesus, of course, fulfilled the function of the prophet to

Israel as well as other functions in his ministry as Messiah. Christians were sympathetic to the role of prophecy, and Agabus functioned in that role on this occasion. He warned that severe famine was ahead for the entire world. "Over all the world" was a characteristic Eastern manner of expression to say with emphasis that the famine would be widespread. A famine came to Judea during the time of Claudius, around A.D. 46, which corresponds to Agabus's warning.

11:29–30. Christians at Antioch wanted to assist Christians in Jerusalem. So the Antioch church decided to set aside contributions, each member as he or she had ability, in order to aid their brothers and sisters in their great distress. Barnabas and Saul became leaders at the Antioch church, and so the church chose them to lead in delivering the offering.

The offering encouraged the Christians at Jerusalem in at least two ways. First, the act affirmed to the Jerusalem church that they were not alone in their circumstances. Second, the offering provided real relief for the basic necessities of life.

For those in trouble, both aspects of encouragement are so important in meeting their needs. The cooperative effort of the two churches made them stronger together than they were separately. This is so important in our missions work, both locally and with Christians separated by distance. One of the hallmarks for Baptists has been our cooperative efforts to meet human need, which is a tremendous witness to Jesus and his love.

Focusing on the Meaning

When the church preaches and lives the redemptive love of Jesus, it will find needs to be met in Jesus' name, and needs will find the church. One small church, for example, as one way of ministering to people's needs in Christ's name, takes up an offering once a month at the Lord's Supper service for those in need. A benevolence committee receives requests for help and responds as the offering permits. It is surprising how, over time, the church has become aware of so many people in need of help and how so many people have been helped. Stated another way, if we are being the church, we will find needs, and they will find us.

The Holy Spirit, God in his presence with us, will help us meet the needs we encounter. A reading of these first chapters of Acts that we have studied so far brings to our attention the several times that the disciples were filled with the Spirit as they encountered an issue or need (see Acts 2:4; 4:8, 31; 6:5). They had an equipping preparation for the task. Notice also, however, that this happened as they acted or were determined to act. God meets us with what we need when we act in his will.

The church considered the somewhat unspectacular act of distributing food as worthy of the church's careful attention. While they wanted to avoid controversy between the Hellenists and the Hebrews (6:1), they showed the seriousness of the task by getting the church involved in solving the challenge as well as setting apart those chosen by the laying on of hands. We do need to watch our motivations for what we do, but work done to meet the needs of others, however menial, is befitting of Jesus' church. So the lesson brings the question to us today: *What need is before us that we are called to meet and consequently be a witness to the goodness, mercy, and salvation of Christ?*

TEACHING PLANS

Teaching Plan—Varied Learning Activities

Connect with Life

1. Prior to the day of the class session, select two learners to assist in presenting the lesson. Each helper will have his or her own part of the lesson to guide. Be sure to make your selection of helpers early. Also, make sure that they have a copy of the *Study Guide* and, if possible, the "Bible Comments" section in this *Teaching Guide* to help them understand, clarify, and explain biblical material for the lesson. Encourage each of your helpers to prepare a short and simple handout for the lesson. Assure both of them that you will be available to help them.

2. At the beginning of class, ask learners whether there are any praise reports or prayer requests regarding the life application from lesson four. Lead the class in prayer. Remember those who spoke up for praise reports and prayer requests.

3. Direct learners to partner with one other person. Instruct them to share with each other information about a human need situation they may know about (natural disaster, loss of home, job, death of loved one, sickness, hunger, etc.). Allow some learners to share these situations with the entire class.

4. Share with learners that today we're going to see how the early church ministered to human need and how we might follow this marvelous pattern set by the early church. Inform the class that today they are blessed to have two helpers to assist you in leading the study. Introduce your helpers by name, and lead the class in applauding for them.

Guide Bible Study

5. Refer to the *Study Guide* and the "Bible Comments" section in this *Teaching Guide* to understand, clarify, and explain biblical material for the lesson.

6. Call on your first helper. The helper should read and summarize Acts 6:1–4. The helper should then explain who the "Hellenists" and the "Hebrews" were. Finally, the helper should explain the historical background to caring for widows and the "daily distribution of food."

7. Lead a guided discussion focusing on this question: *What leadership lessons can we glean from how the apostles handled this crisis?*

8. Summarize briefly Acts 6:8—8:1; 11:19–26 to help learners understand how Christians got to Antioch.

9. Call on your second helper. The helper should read and summarize Acts 11:27–30. The helper should then explain and emphasize how the early church ministered to human need.

10. Thank both of your helpers for their diligence and faithfulness in ministering to the class today. Lead the class in applauding for them.

Encourage Application

11. Divide the white space of a marker board in half by drawing a line down the middle. At the top of the left half of the marker board write the statement, "I can." At the top of the right half of the marker board write the statement, "The church can."

12. Instruct learners to consider the human need stories they heard at the beginning of class. Lead the class in brainstorming what they can possibly do individually in ministering to human needs. Then lead them in brainstorming what your church can possibly do to minister to human needs.

13. Direct learners to consider the list and to write down one thing they will do this week to minister to a human need.

14. End class by praying for human needs and for faithfulness to carry out their commitment.

Teaching Plan—Lecture and Questions

Connect with Life

1. Encourage learners to share praise reports or prayer requests about how they successfully practiced the application from lesson four or how they struggled in practicing it. Pray for them and for application of this lesson.

2. Share with learners a time when you were in need of human assistance (money, housing, transportation, job, health, etc.). How was the situation resolved? Allow several learners to share their own personal experiences. Alternatively, you may share with learners a time when you recognized a human need and worked to meet it in

some way. How was the situation resolved? Allow several learners to share their own personal experiences.

3. Ask, *What do you believe is the church's responsibility in ministering to human needs?*

4. Display the following outline from the *Study Guide*:

- Address the Crisis and Make a Plan (6:1–4)
- Selecting the Seven (6:5–7)
- Love One Another (11:27–30)

5. Refer to the Study Aim for this lesson in the *Study Guide*.

Guide Bible Study

6. Refer to the *Study Guide* and the "Bible Comments" section in this *Teaching Guide* to understand, clarify, and explain biblical material throughout the lesson.

7. Enlist a volunteer to read Acts 6:1–4. Summarize the passage. Then discuss the distinction between the "Hellenists" and the "Hebrews." Also explain the historical background of caring for widows.

8. Lead class in guided discussion focusing on these questions: *Which ministry do you feel is more important according to Scripture—ministering the word of God or meeting human needs? How does this passage address the dilemma? What leadership lessons can we glean from how the apostles handled the crisis?*

9. Invite a volunteer to read Acts 6:5–7. Summarize the passage. Emphasize how the church's response to human needs led to a new way of doing ministry. Lead the class in guided discussion about possible opportunities for the class or church to minister to human needs.

10. Have a volunteer read Acts 11:27–30. Briefly explain how Christians got to Antioch (Acts 6:8—8:1; 11:19–26). Summarize the passage.

Explain "prophets" in the New Testament (11:27) as well as the phrase "in the reign of Claudius" (11:28).

11. Read Acts 11:29. Lead the class in a discussion on how the church can minister to those in need who do not live nearby. Refer to and ask question 5 in the *Study Guide*.

Encourage Application

12. Direct learners to sit quietly and to close their eyes. Instruct them to think about a particular human need situation. Ask this question: *What will you do about that situation this week?*

13. End the class by praying for learners' faithfulness to carry out their commitment.

FOCAL TEXT
Acts 6:8—7:5, 9–28,
35–41, 44–60

BACKGROUND
Acts 6:8—7:60

MAIN IDEA
Stephen challenged accepted
views and practices as
he proclaimed Jesus.

QUESTION TO EXPLORE
What accepted views and
practices are keeping us from
communicating the message
of Jesus to all people?

TEACHING AIM
To lead the class to describe
how Stephen's message
challenged accepted views
and practices and to identify
views and practices that
may be keeping us from
communicating the gospel
of Jesus to all people

LESSON SIX

Challenge Accepted Views for Jesus' Sake

BIBLE COMMENTS

Understanding the Context

For the young church of Jerusalem and Pentecost, their first days were filled with excitement and a sense of change. They had reason to believe that change would sweep across Jerusalem, all of Judea, all of Samaria, and beyond. After all, that was the charge given them by Jesus, to be witnesses to the geographical ends of the earth beginning in Jerusalem (Acts 1:8). And change happened. But soon people of power and beliefs long established raised up in opposition and violent resistance to the change. That resistance began in earnest with Stephen. The church found that change is hard and does not come without suffering and other costs.

Stephen, probably a fairly young man, was passionate about his new-found faith in Christ. We know nothing of his initial experience with Christ. He probably was among the many who accepted Jesus as the Messiah, or Christ, at the preaching of the disciples at Pentecost, or perhaps he was one of the disciples in the upper room (Acts 1:12–15). He appears on the scene of history for one brief but shining moment, and then he goes the way of martyrdom. As far as we know, he was the first Christian martyr.

We met Stephen in the previous lesson. Apparently established as a leader already, he was the first among those selected to distribute resources of the church to the widows. The text characterizes him as one "full of faith and the Holy Spirit" (6:5). To be so filled was to be prepared for the tasks ahead of him. Apparently, through the witness given to him in the Spirit, he responded with faith. Faith for Stephen, as we shall follow him in this lesson, was something one did. Such faith involves belief, or trust, but in Christ and by the Spirit one lives out in all relationships the content of the belief. An active faith is quite different from simply accepting a set of propositions as a statement of belief and holding to those only intellectually.

Interpreting the Scriptures

Standing for Jesus (6:8–10)

6:8. Jesus, the one crucified and now the resurrected Lord, was at the center of matters in Jerusalem at the moment. Stephen, a highly visible witness, was "full of grace and power," attributes he had because of his relationship to Christ. The grace given manifested itself in that he knew what to say and how to say it. The power given was the strength to do so in a circumstance where he and what he gave witness to might be strongly rejected by religious culture and practice. He was prepared to stand for the truth even if it went against accepted views.

6:9–10. People, however, were not ready to let go of their protected and long-held traditions. The "Freedmen" began to debate him. These were descendants of former Roman slaves, perhaps Jews and proselytes, who had their own synagogue as did the other opponents mentioned. They debated Stephen but could not meet what he proclaimed with successful argument.

The Storm Clouds Gather (6:11–15)

6:11. Since Stephen's opponents did not win the argument, they resorted to other means to silence Stephen and stifle the Jesus movement. So they began to instigate false charges against him by manipulating people. The first charge was that of blasphemy, an act of dishonoring or disrespecting both Moses and God. The reference to Moses included the dishonoring of the law that came through Moses.

6:12. Their accusations pushed the emotional hot buttons among the various groups of Jews in Jerusalem. The elders and the scribes, those in authority over Mosaic law and its correct application, got involved in the matter. They compelled Stephen to stand before the council, the Sanhedrin, the high court among the Jews.

6:13–15. "They set up false witnesses." Those against him needed several witnesses although the court normally required just two witnesses for an accusation to be considered. The witnesses added an additional element to the false accusation: Stephen advocated destruction of "this place," referring to the temple. Therefore, Stephen's accusers placed him as one who advocated violence against the two most sacred entities of Judaism, the law and the temple.

6:15. The dramatic moment came as all eyes fixed on Stephen. Such dishonoring of God, the law, and the temple confounded the council. The presence of God was with Stephen, because his face was "like the face of an angel" (6:15). But, how could such things as Stephen said be said in Jerusalem, and indeed, how could his opponents continue to allow such blasphemy? Yet Stephen knew that in what he said was both their hope and salvation, and so he had to say it and did not shrink from the task.

The Storm Begins (7:1)

The high priest, presiding over the court, gave Stephen an opportunity to defend himself. Stephen had an overall defense strategy in his presentation; he followed some of the principal figures through Israel's history and their relationship to God's people. God acted to deliver his people, but Israel often resisted the very deliverance God offered them although God delivered them time and time again. Now his accusers engaged in the same activity by rejecting Jesus.

The Case of Abraham (7:2–5)

Stephen began with Abraham, for Abraham was the father of the Jewish people. God called Abraham from his land in order to lead him to another land (see Genesis 12). Abraham never received the land, "not even a foot's length" (Acts 7:5), but those Stephen addressed were his descendants living in that land at that time. The point is that Abraham received both the call and promise from God in a land quite apart from the land of Israel. So, God does not confine himself to a temple but works in every land.

The Case of Joseph (7:9–16)

7:9–13. Joseph's brothers sold him into slavery because of their jealousy of him (see Gen. 37—46). Joseph landed in Egypt, where he became a leading administrator for the pharaoh. When Joseph's family found themselves in famine conditions, Jacob sent the brothers to Egypt, where there was food.

7:14–16. On the brothers' second visit, Joseph revealed that he was their brother whom they had sold into slavery many years before. Joseph helped to establish the people of Israel in the land of Egypt. The ancestors of Stephen's accusers not only received famine relief, but they also received God's deliverance in a foreign land. Perhaps Stephen also intended to draw a parallel between Joseph and Jesus. Just as Joseph's brothers rejected him and he became their deliverer, so now Jesus' brothers (his fellow Jews) were rejecting him who would be their deliverer if they would accept the truth.

The Case of Moses (7:17–29)

7:17–22. The people of God, living in Egypt and not in the land promised to them, prospered. But then another pharaoh came to rule and brought hardship on the people. Moses, in the meantime, grew to adulthood as the adopted son of Pharaoh's daughter. Moses learned the wisdom of Egypt and became a person known for "his words and deeds" (7:22). God prepared Moses in that land, not the Holy Land, to lead Israel out of its harsh oppression by the new Egyptian ruler. Just as God worked in another land to deliver the people, so Stephen would make the point that God is not confined to a house (the temple) that human hands make (see 7:49–50).

7:23–29. Moses later attempted to identify with his people, the people of Israel, which led him to kill an Egyptian who abused a Hebrew slave. Later, trying to settle a dispute between two Hebrews, the two rejected him and accused him of murder. Moses fled into another land, Midian, in order to avoid any reprisals coming to him for the murder. Like Moses, Jesus was rejected.

7:35–41. Stephen recounted Moses' leading of Israel out of Egypt into the wilderness. It was in that wilderness that Moses revealed that God would raise up a "prophet" for them as Moses himself had been raised up (7:37). Obviously, Stephen pointed toward Jesus in this reference.

But even with the law, or "living oracles" (7:38), and the promise of a prophet, the people rebelled against God and Moses and made a "calf" to worship (7:41).

7:44–50. The "tent of testimony" (7:44), their place of worship designed and built by Moses as God directed, was no stationary structure. They moved it from place to place from the time of Moses up to the time of Solomon, who built the first stationary place of worship. As Stephen continued he quoted from Isaiah 66:1–2 in Acts 7:49 to stress that God "does not dwell in houses made with human hands" (7:48). The whole world is God's, and he is not confined to one place.

The Storm in Full Force (7:51–60)

The accusers became the accused in Stephen's argument. He demonstrated that Israel rejected God time and time again in their history. Now, his accusers were at it again. They were "stiff-necked" (7:51), with hearts and ears closed to the Holy Spirit, just as their fathers before them.

Stephen's harsh but true criticism enraged his accusers and spurred them to mob action. He had a vision of the triumphant and reigning Jesus "at the right hand of God" (7:56) as they stoned him to death. They rejected his true testimony and killed him, much as they did Jesus, who is the truth.

Focusing on the Meaning

The truth is that Jesus fulfilled the temple and the law. In his life, death, and resurrection, he became the temple, the dwelling place of God (see John 2:19). He himself made the law full (see Matt. 5:17). Stephen was the first to begin to stress the universality of Jesus. Jesus is the Savior for everyone in every place if people see him as truth and accept him.

Stephen told the truth, and the people rejected his testimony. Persecution broke out against Christ's people, and they scattered. The gospel of Jesus was on the move and would spread to nations, places, and people all over the world as the good news continues to do today.

Stephen was open to the truth and accepted it while the people as a whole did not, although many did. The question is, *Will we have the attitude of Stephen and be open to the truth?* We never stop growing in Christ, and he will continually challenge us.

The way to know that growth is upon us is to always keep Jesus at the center as Stephen did. His accusers would not move away from the temple and the traditions of the law as their center. They wanted to shape Jesus according to those views and loyalties rather than being loyal to him. Consequently they missed it just as their forefathers missed God's revelation before them. What is it that we are blinded to about ourselves and our culture? Materialism? Racial, class, or cultural prejudice? Radical individualism rather than the corporate body of Christ? Making our mission someone else's responsibility? Inadequate views and understandings about Jesus? It is best to place ourselves corporately and individually in the full light of Jesus and find our answers there. Are we willing to challenge wrongly accepted views, change ourselves, and help others change for the sake of Jesus?

TEACHING PLANS

Teaching Plan—Varied Learning Activities

Connect with Life

1. With this lesson, plan to play the role of Stephen giving his testimony as described in Acts 6:1–15. For maximum impact, dress in costume and act in a manner consistent with Stephen's personality as seen in Acts. If dressing in costume is not possible, then dress in contemporary clothing that Stephen might wear if he were to visit the twenty-first century. An alternative to this is to enlist a volunteer to play the role of Stephen. Another alternative is to play the role of Adina (a fictitious character), one of the Hellenistic Jewish widows discussed in Acts 6:1 who testifies about the ministry of Stephen. Yet another option might be to enlist a volunteer to play

the role of Adina. The rest of the lesson plan assumes that you will play the role of Stephen.

2. Refer to the *Study Guide* and the "Bible Comments" section in this *Teaching Guide* to understand, clarify, and explain biblical material throughout the lesson.

3. Enlist a volunteer to place a copy of the lesson handout, "Accepted Views and Practices," in each learner's chair prior to class beginning. The lesson handout is available in "Teaching Resource Items" for this study at www.baptistwaypress.org.

4. Instruct the volunteer to announce that you won't be teaching the lesson today. The volunteer should then ask learners whether there are praise reports or prayer requests regarding life application from the last lesson. The volunteer should pray for the class and the lesson experience. He or she should be sure to remember those who spoke up for praise reports and prayer requests.

5. The volunteer should introduce Stephen using these words: *I am honored to introduce a man who is known around the world as a faithful servant and courageous soldier for our Lord. Like our service men and women who put their lives on the line for our freedom, this man has been the poster child for boldness in the body of Christ. He is here today to share his story. So let's welcome my friend and your brother Stephen.*

6. Share your testimony as Stephen. End the Stephen testimony by thanking the class for the opportunity to share with them. At this point you may assume your regular role as teacher or allow the volunteer to guide the rest of the lesson. The following instructions assume you will direct the lesson.

Guide Bible Study

7. Enlist a volunteer to read Acts 6:1–15. Direct learners to form groups of two to four people. Instruct learners to identify and discuss the personal and ministry traits of Stephen. Ask: *What does the life and ministry of Stephen teach us about God? What does the life and ministry of Stephen teach us about people? What does the*

life and ministry of Stephen teach us about life? Allow some groups to report their findings.

8. Direct learners to reconvene with their groups. Ask: *How would you describe the adversaries of Stephen? Why?* Allow some groups to report their findings.

9. Direct learners to reconvene with their groups. Enlist a volunteer to read Acts 7:1–5, 9–28. Invite a second volunteer to read Acts 7:35–41. Have a third volunteer read Acts 7:44–60.

10. Lead learners to describe and discuss Stephen's message and its result. Ask: *What do Stephen's message and its result teach us about God? What do Stephen's message and its result teach us about people? What does Stephen's message and its result teach us about life?*

Encourage Application

11. Direct class attention to the lesson handout. Instruct participants to consider their relationships with friends, relatives, associates (business partners, employees, employers, doctor, mechanic, etc.) and neighbors.

12. Instruct learners to record accepted views and practices held by those in the "Relationship" column that may be keeping them from communicating the gospel of Jesus Christ.

13. End class by asking God to give learners the courage to overcome the accepted views and practices recorded on the lesson handout.

Lesson Handout: Accepted Views and Practices

Relationships	Accepted Views & Practices
Friends	
Relatives	
Associates	
Neighbors	

Teaching Plan—Lecture and Questions

Connect with Life

1. Prior to class beginning, place a copy of the lesson handout, "Challenge Accepted Views for Jesus' Sake," in the chair of each learner. The lesson handout is the partially completed outline of the lesson. The lesson handout is available in "Teaching Resource Items" for this study at www.baptistwaypress.org.

2. Lead learners to share praise reports or prayer requests about how they successfully practiced the application from the last lesson or how they struggled in trying to put the application into practice. Pray for them and for this study session.

3. Begin class by recalling a time when you were a kid and you gave in to peer pressure. Allow several learners to share their own childhood peer pressure experience.

4. Share with the class that in today's lesson we witness someone standing strong against accepted views and practices.

Guide Bible Study

5. Refer to the *Study Guide* and the "Bible Comments" section in this *Teaching Guide* to understand, clarify, and explain biblical material throughout the lesson.

6. Direct learners' attention to the part of the lesson handout that focuses on "Irrefutable Witness." Enlist a volunteer to read Acts 6:8–15.

7. Instruct learners to write the word *Ministry* in the first blank under the topic heading "Irrefutable Witness."

8. Discuss Acts 6:1–15. Point out that Stephen was not one of the apostles but was one of the seven selected to take care of the distribution of food. Ask, *Why was Stephen opposed?* Then ask, *What message does this send to you about serving God?* Share with them a time

when you or someone you know was opposed because of service to God.

9. Instruct learners to write the word *Message* in the second blank under the topic heading "Irrefutable Witness." Enlist a volunteer to read Acts 7:1–5. Enlist a second volunteer to read Acts 7:9–28. Enlist a third volunteer to read Acts 7:35–41 and a fourth volunteer to read Acts 7:44–60. Discuss these passages, focusing on (1) God's work with Israel and (2) Israel's rebellion against God. Also explain Stephen's concluding challenge.

10. Ask: *How did Stephen confront the false assumptions of those who questioned him? What can we learn from Stephen about how to address false assumptions that we face?*

11. Direct learners' attention to the part of the lesson handout that focuses on "Incarnational and Sacrificial Witness." Enlist a volunteer to read Acts 7:54–60.

12. Instruct learners to write the word *Persecuted* in the first blank under the topic heading "Incarnational and Sacrificial Witness." Summarize verses 54–58. Explain that Stephen's adversaries sought to protect the law and the temple. Ask, *What do legalists even in our churches today seek to protect?*

13. Instruct learners to write the word *Praying* in the last blank under the topic heading "Incarnational and Sacrificial Witness." Summarize verses 59–60. Ask: *How was Stephen like Jesus in his death? What lessons should we learn from this?*

Encourage Application

14. Ask the class to name some current accepted views and practices that may keep them from communicating the gospel. Refer to and summarize "Implications and Actions" in the *Study Guide* as seems helpful.

15. End the class by praying and asking God to address the views and practices that prevent us from sharing the gospel.

Lesson Handout

Challenge Accepted Views for Jesus' Sake

Stephen challenged the accepted views and practices as he proclaimed Jesus.

I. Irrefutable Witness (Acts 6:8—7:5, 9–28, 44–53)

    A. Stephen's _____ (6:8–15)

    B. Stephen's _____ (7:1–5, 9–28, 44–53)

II. Incarnational and Sacrificial Witness (Acts 7:54–60)

    A. Stephen_____ (7:54–58)

    B. Stephen_____ (7:59–60)

FOCAL TEXT
Acts 8:26–40

BACKGROUND
Acts 8:4–40

MAIN IDEA
Responding to the leading
of the Spirit, Philip told
the inquirer the good
news about Jesus.

QUESTION TO EXPLORE
How can we be more
sensitive and responsive to
the leading of God's Spirit
in sharing the gospel?

TEACHING AIM
To lead participants to describe
the conversation of Philip and
the Ethiopian and to identify
ways to be more responsive
to the leading of God's Spirit
in sharing the gospel

LESSON SEVEN

Be Available to God's Spirit to Share the Gospel

BIBLE COMMENTS

Understanding the Context

The first stage in the founding of the New Testament church was the establishment of a large group of faithful believes in Jerusalem (Acts 1—6). The second stage was for believers to be witnesses of Christ in Judea and Samaria, and "to the ends of the earth" (Acts 1:8).[1] God accomplished the continuing growth of the church beyond Jerusalem by means of a severe persecution of Christians in Jerusalem, in which God used Stephen and Philip, among others.

Stephen and Philip were not among the twelve apostles of Christ. Rather, they were part of the group of seven men who were chosen to help bring order to the church in Jerusalem so that the apostles could focus on prayer and preaching (Acts 6). These "seven" were expected to be wise and Spirit-controlled. Stephen and Philip were also gifted in preaching the good news of Jesus.

The persecution of the church began when false charges of religious heresy were brought against Stephen (6:11–14). Stephen responded with a remarkable testimony about Jesus. His words were twisted against him, and he was stoned to death. At the place of Stephen's death was a young man named Saul, who would soon become an unrelenting persecutor of God's people (8:1–3; 9:1). Saul later became known as the Apostle Paul.

After Stephen's death many Christians were forced to leave Jerusalem. The terror of persecution, though, did not silence their voices. One of these displaced Christians was Philip, who was willing for God to use him to share with others the life-changing story of Jesus Christ.

Philip first preached to the people of Samaria, which was scandalous to early Christians from a Jewish background. For many centuries Samaritans and Jews had little to do with one another. Samaria was located between Galilee and Judea. This area had once been called the Northern kingdom of Israel until it was captured by the Assyrians in 721 B.C. Most of the Jewish population was taken away as slaves at that time. This area was re-populated with non-Jews, thus producing a citizenry that was only partly Jewish at best. Most Jews would not even walk through Samaria. Samaritans were considered beyond the boundaries of God's love.

When Philip reported Samaritans were being saved, the apostles in Jerusalem sent Peter and John to investigate (Acts 8:14–17). However, God did not stop with the Samaritans. The good news was soon taken to an entirely different continent because of Philip's availability to the Holy Spirit and his willingness to go beyond his comfort zone.

Interpreting the Scriptures

Availability to the Spirit (8:26–31)

8:26. Perhaps Philip's first gift as an evangelist was his willingness to be available to God in sharing the good news about Jesus. After Philip's successful ministry in Samaria, an angel told him to travel south from Jerusalem to Gaza. The old city of Gaza, located on the southern coast of the Mediterranean Sea in Philistia, had been destroyed in 93 B.C. A newer Gaza was built south of the old city about thirty-five years later. Rome constructed a harbor for ships at the new city, thus increasing trade and traffic along the main road that ran from Gaza to Jerusalem, a distance of about sixty miles. However, more than one road meandered from Jerusalem south toward Gaza. The Holy Spirit's directions to Philip had to be specific. Philip likely found the Ethiopian north of Gaza, where enough water was available in this desert country for his baptism.

8:27–28. Philip quickly discovered the Holy Spirit's focus on the Gaza road was a eunuch who was a trusted government official, the treasurer of the queen of Ethiopia. Eunuchs were often used as court officials. Candace was not a personal name but a title. The country of Ethiopia at this time was the region we now call Sudan, and was considered by many Jews (and others) to be the "ends of the earth" beyond which people could not live. Many commentators believe this Ethiopian was a black African, but they have varying opinions on whether he was a Jew (either born or a proselyte) or a non-Jewish *God-fearer* (a Gentile who respected the Jewish faith and participated as much as possible in Jewish worship).

Old Testament references to eunuchs include Deuteronomy 23:1 and Isaiah 56:3–5. This nobleman appeared to have recently attended a religious gathering in Jerusalem and was returning home. Perhaps his experience at the temple had stirred his heart to seek more of God. Philip found him reading from God's word. During the early years of the establishment of the Israelites in Canaan, eunuchs were not allowed to "enter the assembly of the LORD" (Deut. 23:1). Many Bible commentators believe that eunuchs were not allowed in the temple (beyond a certain restricted area) in the time of Christ and beyond. This Ethiopian eunuch wanted to know more of God, but his search for God had been thwarted by religious and cultural barriers. Philip had to leave his comfort zone to overcome these barriers.

8:29–31. Philip's availability to the Holy Spirit may have placed him at great personal risk since court officials likely were protected by bodyguards. Philip literally "ran" to the carriage and heard the eunuch reading from the prophet Isaiah. (Reading in ancient times was usually aloud.) The Ethiopian's reply to Philip's question (Acts 8:30) indicated the Holy Spirit had already prepared his heart. The Ethiopian had no false pride or pretense of knowledge or personal righteousness. Instead, he was eager to hear about Jesus. Philip was available to God for this holy purpose.

The Suffering Servant (8:32–33)

The eunuch was reading from Isaiah 53:7–8. Most Jews thought of the Messiah as a conquering hero who would overthrow foreign powers ruling over Israel and establish God's kingdom by force. Almost no one believed the promised Messiah would come as a suffering servant. Jesus himself changed the imagery of the true Messiah from that of a military-like ruler to a servant (see Matthew 8:17; 20:25–28; Philippians 3:10; 1 Peter 1:10–11; 4:12–13). Jesus lived and died as a servant in order to reveal the depth of God's love for his creation and to offer the gift of salvation to all who would receive it (Philippians 2:6–11; Ephesians 1:7). Jesus was the suffering servant of Isaiah 53.

The Power of the Spirit (8:34–38)

8:34. Philip understood that Isaiah was talking about Jesus. Because Jesus applied these verses to himself, early Christians also read them that way (see Mark 10:45; Luke 22:37; 24:20; John 1:29; 12:27; Acts 3:13–14; Romans 4:25; Hebrews 9:26–28; 1 Peter 2: 21–25).

8:35. Philip began the story of Jesus at the point of the Ethiopian's interest and need. The New Testament did not yet exist. The prophetic voice of Isaiah had been fulfilled in the sacrificial life, death, burial, and resurrection of Jesus Christ.

8:36. Philip's passionate, knowledgeable, and yet simple testimony about Jesus was Spirit-directed and effective. Part of Philip's witness about Jesus certainly would have been that each believer should repent of his or her sins, be baptized in water, and receive the Holy Spirit. The historic fact of Jesus' suffering and death for our sins was used by the Holy Spirit to bring the nobleman to faith in Christ, for he asked Philip to baptize him.[2] The eunuch had been considered unworthy or unfit to approach near to God in the temple. Would this same prohibition keep him away from Christ? Was grace alone, through faith alone, sufficient for his salvation? Could anything keep him from the love of Christ? (See Rom. 8:35–39; John 3:16–17.)

8:38. Both Philip and the eunuch "went down into the water." The word *baptize* means *to cover completely* or *to fully immerse*. The focus of the verse is on the eunuch's salvation, though. Baptism is the outward symbol of an inward transformation.

The Personal Prompting of the Spirit (8:39–40)

As quickly as the Holy Spirit led Philip to the Ethiopian, the Spirit led Philip away, and "the eunuch . . . went on his way rejoicing." The eunuch's joy was not about Philip but about Christ, who was now the Ethiopian's companion on his long journey home.

Philip had other Spirit-led work to do. Azotus was the same city as ancient Ashdod. Philip apparently followed the coast road north. He preached the good news along the way until he reached Caesarea, where he made his home.

Philip is mentioned twenty years later (Acts 21:8–9) when Luke and Paul stayed at Philip's home. Philip had four unmarried daughters who all "prophesied" (preached the gospel).

Focusing on the Meaning

The opportunity to share our faith is one of our most joyous privileges as Christians. Most twenty-first century American Christians live in communities filled with churches. We can easily assume everyone knows about Jesus. My experience tells me this is not true.

I met Jonathan when he was the manager of a business with which I had dealings. One day I felt impressed to speak to Jonathan about the Christian faith. He discovered I was a pastor. He seemed sincerely happy I was there. He had been secretly hoping someone could tell him about Christ and involve his family in a good church. A couple of months later Jonathan was baptized. He and his family became active members of our church.

Jonathan and I first began talking about Jesus because we were both praying. I was praying I could share my faith with someone, and he was praying someone would share the gospel with him. At a pivotal time in his life Jonathan needed to hear about Jesus. The Holy Spirit directed me to speak to him during that time. The Holy Spirit also had prepared Jonathan's heart.

Jonathan's story, and many others, encourages me to say a word for Jesus as often as I can. Whenever I am prompted to speak about Christ, I have full assurance God has prepared someone to hear about Christ.

I am not as spiritually gifted as Philip. Perhaps you are not, either. However, the calling to share our faith is not primarily about powerful giftedness but personal availability to the Holy Spirit.

A word of caution is in order. Being Spirit-led means God may take us beyond our comfort zone. The gospel is for everyone, including people who are very much unlike us. Philip discovered God is greater than human differences. When we become available to the Holy Spirit, we will make the same discovery.

TEACHING PLANS

Teaching Plan—Varied Learning Activities

Connect with Life

1. Bring to the class session a box, about twelve inches square or larger, that you have covered in plain wrapping paper. With marking pen label one side, "Comfort Zone." As members are gathering, ask them to call out people or situations that make them uncomfortable. (Suggestions: a crowd of strangers; a crowd of people speaking a language other than yours; music that doesn't fit your generation; people behaving in ways different from your cultural background; street people.) Write one suggestion on each of the other five sides of the box.

    Explain that the box illustrates our *comfort zone*—the place we feel secure and confident. The sides of the box are walls or boundaries we have built for ourselves. Often we feel insecure trying to witness to people who are outside our *box*—our safe zone. The problem is, many of the people we need to reach for Christ are beyond our boundaries. Refer to and read Quick Read and Question to Explore for this lesson in the *Study Guide.* Place the box at the visual center of this study.

Guide Bible Study

2. Explore the life of Philip through three research teams. Write out these assignments for the teams. Allow teams about five minutes to prepare brief reports:
    *   *Team 1:* Study Acts 6:1–7, and summarize why Philip was qualified to be one of the seven selected to serve.
    *   *Team 2:* Study Acts 8:1, 4–7, and summarize why Philip was found witnessing in Samaria.
    *   *Team 3:* Study Acts 21:7–9, and describe Philip about twenty years later when Paul visited him on his way home from the third missionary journey.

(A copy of the assignments is available in "Teaching Resource Items" for this study at www.baptistwaypress.org.)

Call for brief reports, and emphasize these findings:
- Philip was filled with the Holy Spirit and responsive to his leading.
- When persecution drove Philip from Jerusalem, he took the gospel message to Samaria.
- Philip was an enthusiastic and effective witness wherever he went.
- Philip settled in Caesarea and raised a godly family there.

3. Lead a conversational reading of Acts 8:26–31, using the Scripture passage printed in the *Study Guide*. Assign someone to read the quoted words of the Holy Spirit (8:26, 29); a second person to read for Philip (8:30): and a third to read for the Ethiopian (8:31). Enlist a narrator to read everything that is not in quotation marks. After the reading, ask, *How does a person become sensitive and responsive to the voice and leading of the Holy Spirit, as Philip was?* Encourage group members to share ways they seek and determine the Spirit's leading in their lives. Add suggestions from the small article, "Discerning the Prompting of the Holy Spirit," in the *Study Guide*.

4. Briefly share information on Ethiopia and the eunuch from the *Study Guide* sections, "People Need to Know about Jesus," "The Spirit Leads beyond Our Boundaries," and the small article, "Ethiopia."

5. Ask the person who was reading for the Ethiopian man to read Acts 8:32–35. Follow with these questions:
- Why is it important for us to know and use Scripture in witnessing?
- How did Philip keep Jesus central in his witnessing?
- What barriers do you think Philip had to cross as he climbed up into the Ethiopian's chariot? (Mention place, language, culture, religious traditions, social status, and the unknown.)

Encourage Application

6. Propose a two-week *Philip Project,* to help everyone become bolder
    and more focused in witnessing. Give out slips of paper, and ask
    them to list three names of people in their worlds who probably
    have not yet received Christ as Savior. (Suggest extended family
    members, neighbors, work associates, and old high school buddies
    as possibilities for their lists.) Agree together to pray daily that God
    will open an opportunity for them to share their own story of con-
    version with one of these people. Form small groups and encourage
    members to share their lists and pray for each other. Plan to share
    Philip Project testimonies during the next two sessions.

Teaching Plan—Lecture and Questions

Connect with Life

1. Open with the story of the church that reached out to an undocu-
    mented immigrant, at the beginning of this lesson. Acknowledge
    that the story raises issues on which we may not all agree. Ask,
    *What risks did those church members take when they chose to wit-
    ness to that man?* Invite members to share similar experiences they
    may have had in reaching out to *outsiders,* people beyond their
    comfort zones.

2. Read the Main Idea, Quick Read, and Question to Explore for this
    lesson from the *Study Guide.* Lead the group to begin a list on the
    markerboard titled, "Ways to Hear and Respond to the Holy Spirit."

Guide Bible Study

3. Provide a brief vignette of the life of Philip, based on Acts 6:1–7;
    8:1–7. Find help in the *Study Guide* section, "People Need to Know
    about Jesus."

4. Call for someone to read Acts 8:26–31. Using a map of the New
    Testament world in the time of Paul, locate these places:

- Samaria, where Philip was living
- The area of Samaria in relation to Jerusalem
- The road between Jerusalem and Gaza where this encounter took place
- Ethiopia in Bible times (see *Study Guide* article, "Ethiopia)

5. Ask, *How do you think Philip heard and followed the leading of the Spirit?* Add any new suggestions to the list begun in step two. Ask a member to read aloud the *Study Guide* article, "Discerning the Prompting of the Holy Spirit." Then add additional suggestions to the board.

6. On markerboard draw an equilateral triangle (a triangle in which all three sides are equal). Label the top point, "Holy Spirit." Label the two bottom points, "Philip" and "The Ethiopian." Explain the illustration in terms like these:
   - The Holy Spirit of God is primary to success in any witnessing situation.
   - The Spirit works both to empower the Christian to witness (Philip), and to prepare the heart of the one who needs to hear about Jesus (the Ethiopian).
   - A witnessing situation often waits on the Christian to sense the Spirit's leading and open interaction with the seeker.
   - Successful witnessing does not require coercion, because the Spirit is the Mover, and the Christian simply shares the gospel.

   Read Acts 8:32–35 as the group listens for how that triangle worked in Philip's experience. Using the background section, "The Spirit Leads Beyond Our Boundaries," emphasize and describe the barriers Philip and the Ethiopian had to overcome in this situation (see step 5 in "Teaching Plan—Varied Learning Activities").

7. Complete the story from Acts 8:36–40. Draw from the last two sections of the lesson in the *Study Guide,* and follow with these questions:
   - How important is baptism for a new believer?
   - How does the eunuch's baptism compare to Jesus' baptism in mode (see Matthew 3:13–16; Mark 1:9–10)?

- Why was it unusual for a non-Jewish eunuch to be accepted as a worshiper of God?
- How did the Ethiopian man feel when he and Philip parted ways?
- What did the Spirit lead Philip to do next?

Encourage Application

8. Ask a member to read the list, "Ways to Hear and Respond to the Holy Spirit." Invite several members to answer, *What can we learn about witnessing from Philip?*

NOTES

1. Unless otherwise indicated, all Scripture quotations in lessons 7–8 are from the HOLY BIBLE, NEW INTERNATIONAL VERSION®. Copyright © 1973, 1978, 1984 Biblica.

2. Some versions of the Bible contain verse 37, in which Philip responds to the Ethiopian's request for baptism by saying, "If you believe with all your heart, you may." Then the nobleman answered, "I believe that Jesus Christ is the Son of God." These words are not found in the most reliable manuscripts and seem to be a later addition, representing the ritual of Christian baptism practiced in the early church. Regardless, Philip was certainly convinced that this high official of the Ethiopian government was genuinely converted to Christ.

FOCAL TEXT
Acts 9:1–22, 26–28

BACKGROUND
Acts 9:1–28

MAIN IDEA
Paul, Christianity's greatest enemy, became the greatest missionary for Christ, with help from Ananias and Barnabas.

QUESTION TO EXPLORE
Who's the most unlikely person to become a Christian whom you know personally?

TEACHING AIM
To lead participants to trace how Paul, Christianity's fiercest opponent, came to be included in the Christian community and become Christianity's greatest missionary, and to identify how God can use them to reach an unlikely person for Christ

LESSON EIGHT
Don't Neglect the Hard Cases

BIBLE COMMENTS

Understanding the Context

Saul may have been the least likely person to become a follower of Christ as the early church grew. However, not only did Saul become a sincere and devoted disciple of Jesus, he became the greatest missionary the church has ever known. Who was Saul?

Saul was a Jew from the city of Tarsus, in the Roman province of Cilicia in southeastern Asia Minor. Cilicia was known for its fine wool and textiles. Saul's professional trade was that of a "tentmaker" (Acts 18:3), one trained in the making and use of textiles. After his conversion, this skill provided for his income (Acts 18:3; 20:34; 1 Thessalonians 2:9; 2 Thessalonians 3:8). Saul also was deeply involved in studying and practicing his Jewish religion (Acts 11:26; Galatians 1:14; Philippians 3:4–6).

Saul's Jewish forefathers may have come to Tarsus when Greece was the dominant world power as part of an effort to increase the city's commercial growth. Later, when Rome became the dominant power, Roman citizenship was granted to all the citizens of Tarsus, including the Jews. Saul could rightly say he was born a citizen of Rome, to the dismay of many non-citizens who sought this high honor (Acts 22:28–29).

A famous university was also at Tarsus. We cannot know for certain whether Saul was a student at the university, but after his conversion his ability to share the gospel reflected his superior knowledge and intellect. Acts 22:3 indicates that he was highly educated in the Jewish law, having been "brought up" in Jerusalem and having studied with the famous rabbi Gamaliel. However, he always relied on the Holy Spirit when he spoke of Christ (1 Corinthians 2:1–10).

Many Christians have not had a *Damascus Road* experience. We may not have seen a blinding light or heard a voice from heaven. However, all true believers have acknowledged their sins, repented of them, and received God's gift of salvation in Christ. Some of us had a friend who invited us into God's circle of grace. Saul's Christian friends were Ananias and Barnabas, and Saul's salvation teaches us to not neglect the hard cases.

Interpreting the Scriptures

Saul's Commission (9:1–2)

9:1. Saul began his persecution of Christians after the death of Stephen (Acts 7:58—8:1). Saul's attacks on Christians were described as "murderous threats," portraying the image of a wild beast ripping apart the flock of God. Saul was "breathing out" (image of *snorting* and *growling*) these threats as he went about the task of rooting out the Christian faith. His misguided religious commission was evil and blinded him to his violation of the sixth commandment (Exodus 20:13).

9:2. Saul was on his way to Damascus, a major city of Syria located about a week's journey north of Jerusalem, to arrest Christians who had managed to elude his grasp in Jerusalem. He obtained "letters" (*warrants*) from the religious authorities. No one (except God) could legally question Saul's right to be morally wrong. Saul's commission was to "destroy the church" (Acts 8:3). He sought to imprison everyone, "whether men or women." No one was exempt from Saul's terror.

Saul's Conversion (9:3–6)

9:3–4. Saul was suddenly and powerfully confronted by the One he was convinced was dead. A blinding light from heaven and a voice that seemed to come from the light stopped him from going farther. Jesus' question confirmed that Saul's persecution of Christians was also a persecution of Christ.

9:5. Saul's question and his prostrate position confirmed that Saul knew he was not in control of this experience. Jesus identified himself as the object of Saul's persecution. Saul seemed to understand quickly that Jesus identified completely with his disciples.

9:6. Although Christ's confrontation of Saul was sudden, Saul's conversion may have come during the next few days through a series of small steps of obedience to Christ. Regardless of exactly when or how, however, Saul was sincerely and fully converted to Christ. He became aware of his sin, repented of it, and opened his heart to God's gift of salvation in Christ. Saul became a new person (Gal. 2:20; Ephesians 2:8–9; Phil. 1:21; 3:7–9; 2 Corinthians 5:17).

We should notice Saul was not seeking a relationship with Christ when he was converted. Details of Saul's salvation experience appear in Acts 9; 22; and 26. Each time the focus is on God's overwhelming grace. However, Saul was not forced against his will to follow Christ, except as all believers are *compelled* by the love of God (2 Cor. 5:14). The great miracle of Saul's conversion was that God's grace was so feely given to one so filled with pride and self-righteousness (Gal. 1:13–14; Romans 3:23; 5:8; 12:2; 1 Cor. 15:9). Each one of us is saved by God's grace, alone (Eph. 2:8–9).

Saul's Challenge (9:7–9)

Saul was temporarily blinded and took no physical nourishment for three days. During this time the Lord undoubtedly spoke to Saul about what God would soon ask him to do, preparing the way for the visit of Ananias. The Lord ministered to Saul as a shepherd cares for one of his sheep (Matthew 18:12–14; Luke 15). These were days of spiritual healing and preparation for Saul. Saul was challenged to trust God completely, even while he was unsure of his future.

Saul's Calling (9:10–22)

9:10–14. Most commentators believe Ananias was a resident of Damascus, not a refugee fleeing from Saul's persecution in Jerusalem. Ananias had been a Christian long enough to have matured somewhat in Christ and was likely a leader of the church in Damascus. Ananias was at first reluctant to respond to the Lord's request to speak to Saul, but his faith in Christ was strong enough to overcome his fears (Isaiah 6:8).

Ananias must have been surprised to hear that Saul was praying and that Saul also had a vision regarding Ananias. Until then, as far as anyone knew, God could have been punishing Saul for his cruel behavior, not offering him salvation through this traumatic experience. God's request of Ananias must have been shocking to the entire Christian community. Ananias was willing to be obedient but not before reminding the Lord that Saul was an evil man who had a legal right to harm

Christians in Damascus. Ananias's obedience could have been perceived as a confrontation with the Jewish authorities of Jerusalem. Both Saul and Ananias had to trust God.

9:15–16. Just as there were special vessels in God's temple, the Lord had chosen Saul for a special purpose in God's kingdom (Romans 1:1; Gal. 1:15). Saul would take the gospel to Gentiles, kings, and all Israel. However his Christian journey would be one of suffering for Christ (Acts 20:22–23).

9:17. Ananias treated Saul with respect. He entered the house of Judas (not Judas Iscariot) and placed his hands on Saul as one would bless a friend. Ananias announced that Saul was now his brother in Christ and that Christ had sent Ananias to minister to Saul. Saul's sins, as grievous as they were, had been completely forgiven by God. He was "filled with the Holy Spirit" (see Acts 22:14–16 for a fuller account of Ananias's words.)

9:18–19. Through Ananias's obedience, God restored Saul's sight. Saul was baptized, and then he took nourishment to regain his physical strength. His experience with Christ had already nourished him spiritually (see John 4:13, 31–32).

9:20–22. The Christians in Damascus began to disciple Saul. He was soon testifying about his conversion, declaring to the Jews in Damascus that "Jesus is the Son of God." This was not merely Christ's title but a description of his true Messianic nature and his factual relationship to God. This Jesus whom Saul encountered was the Savior of the world (Colossians 1:15–20).

The people who heard Saul preach were astonished. They knew he had been authorized to destroy the church. He was now its chief proponent and defender. His words were spoken in the authority of the Holy Spirit, for he powerfully "baffled" them, "proving" (image of *knitting together* all the evidence) that Jesus is indeed the Christ.

Saul's Companions (9:26–28)

9:26–27. The news of Saul's conversion to Christ left him without friends in Jerusalem. The Jews viewed him as a traitor (Acts 9:23), and the Christians believed him to be a deceiver. Ananias had befriended Saul in Damascus, and Barnabas ("Son of Encouragement," Acts 4:36) befriended Saul in Jerusalem. Barnabas introduced Saul to the apostles and explained his call to preach. Saul needed such friends.

9:28. Ultimately, Saul was welcomed into the Christian fellowship of Jerusalem. He continued to preach without fear. Sometime later, Saul turned his attention more fully to the conversion of the Gentiles (13:46–48).

Focusing on the Meaning

Many Christians wonder whether God can use them to reach someone for Christ. What about you? Could God use you to help someone find salvation in Jesus?

I once helped a woman change a flat tire along a busy roadway. Later, I saw her at a funeral service. Only then did she realize a minister had helped her change her tire. Although this woman and her family had not attended church for many years, she told her children they were all going to join my church. "He's a real Christian," she explained. Until that experience she had been hardened against ministers and churches. I am no more real as a Christian than many other believers, but the Holy Spirit softened her heart and allowed me to speak to her about Christ. Until then, she had been a hard case.

Saul also was a hard case. He was not interested in the Christian message. But Ananias and Barnabas were *real* Christians who knew Saul was not beyond the boundaries of God's love. These two Christians became conduits of God's grace to Saul. Saul responded positively to their Christ-like love and personal friendship. They took a chance on Saul, but the Holy Spirit was already at work in Saul's life.

When we follow the example of Ananias and Barnabas, people will know we are followers of Jesus Christ. God will give us opportunities to share our faith. Ananias brought healing and love to Saul. Barnabas introduced Saul to the larger Christian community. Both of these influences in Saul's life were wholesome, positive, and generous in spirit. When the Holy Spirit is at work in our lives, we always have hope that the gospel will produce new believers, even some we might consider to be the hard cases.

TEACHING PLANS

Teaching Plan—Varied Learning Activities

Connect with Life

1. As the group gathers, invite any who tried the "Philip Project" from lesson seven (praying for friends or family who need the Lord, and looking for opportunities to share their story of conversion with them) to tell how the project is working for them. Prompt with: *Did you remember to pray for your people? Did you wait for someone to come to you, or did you initiate a time together with him or her? Were you able to share any of your story of conversion? What might your next step be in building a bridge toward salvation?*

2. Give a copy of this multiple-choice quiz to each person. (A copy is available in "Teaching Resource Items" for this study at www.baptistwaypress.org.)

Reaching the Unlikely Person

(1) Have you ever encountered someone who was working to destroy Christianity?

_____ a radical terrorist?

_____ a member of a militant secular organization?

_____ a skeptical college professor?

_____ a cynical neighbor or work associate?

(2) How did you pray when you realized someone wanted to damage your faith?

_____ that God would protect America?

_____ that God would protect your church?

_____ that God would save that person by his grace?

_____ that God would use you to help bring that person to himself?

Encourage members to huddle in groups of three or four and discuss the options. Reassemble after about three minutes, and read the Quick Read and Question to Explore found at the beginning of the lesson in the *Study Guide*.

Guide Bible Study

3. Review Paul's story from Acts 7:56—8:3, using information found in the *Study Guide* section, "The Miracle of Paul's Conversion." Afterward, ask the group to suggest several reasons Paul was unlikely to ever come to faith in Jesus as Savior and Lord.

4. Divide into two teams. (To encourage participation by all team members, teams should have six or fewer people each. Form additional teams with duplicate assignments if attendance is larger than twelve.) Write on the board Scripture references for the other two accounts of Paul's conversion story, and assign one to each team.

- Acts 22:1–11—Paul's defense when he was arrested in Jerusalem
- Acts 26:9–19—Paul's trial before King Herod Agrippa in Caesarea

Read the Acts 9:1–9 account aloud as the teams search their parallel passages for details added by Paul when he later recounted the amazing event. The Acts 22 team will discover details about Paul's life before conversion. The Acts 26 team will find more facts about Paul's persecution of Christians and about the call of God on his life. Note that Paul's story was a very important part of his later witness to unbelievers.

5. Keep the same teams. Assign one to research the role of Ananias in Paul's conversion (Acts 9:10–19). Assign the other to discover the role of Barnabas in helping believers receive Paul into the churches (Acts 9:20–22, 26–30). Make two columns on the board. As teams report, list words that describe the actions of Ananias and Barnabas. (Suggestions: listening to God, obedient, willing to risk, mentoring, befriending, encouraging, speaking out.)

Encourage Application

6. Refer to the *Study Guide* and read the small article, "Conversion Experience," for the group. Ask, *What is the moment or event you look back to, when Christ revealed himself to you, and you believed in him? Did you have a mentor or an encourager in the early days of your faith?* Invite several to share personal testimonies of salvation. Challenge each person to write his or her story in a concise paragraph and practice telling it aloud, so it will be an available, believable tool when they have opportunities to speak out for Christ.

7. Refer again to the "Philip Project" from lesson seven. Suggest that they add to their list the name of someone who is a *hard case*—a person they think of as unlikely to receive Christ. Note these encouraging facts from today's study:
   - God is able to intervene and touch even the most difficult person.
   - Someone on your "Philip Project" list could become very important in the work of Christ.

Challenge learners to come with experiences to share in the next session.

Teaching Plan—Lecture and Questions

Connect with Life

1. Pose these questions for the group to begin the study.
   - On a global scale, who do you think are Christianity's greatest enemies today?
   - In the United States, what influences are seeking to sideline Christianity?
   - Who is the most unlikely person to become a Christian that you know personally?

2. Read the Main Idea and Quick Read" for this lesson from the *Study Guide.*

Guide Bible Study

3. Begin by summarizing Paul's life before conversion from Acts 7:58—8:3. Find additional insights in the *Study Guide* section, "The Miracle of Paul's Conversion," and in "Understanding the Context" in this *Teaching Guide.* Note that Paul was a highly educated religious leader, very zealous for his faith and sincere in his actions, but sincerely wrong.

4. Call for a reading of Acts 9:1–8. Trace on a map the journey Paul and his companions were making. Note the approximate location of this event—not far from the city of Damascus. Underscore these facts from "The Miracle of Paul's Conversion":
   - Paul thought he was doing God's work in exterminating Christians.
   - Paul's experience was validated in that others saw the light and heard the voice (see Acts 9:7; 22:9).
   - The days of blindness allowed God to get Paul's full attention.

- God is fully able to intervene in any life—however hardened—and effect change.

5. Call on two people to read Acts 9:9–19 conversationally. Ask one to read the narration and the other to read the Lord's quoted words (use the printed Scripture in the *Study Guide*). Guide the group to search more deeply with these questions:
    - What was Ananias's initial reaction to God's request in verses 13–14?
    - What does God's plan for Paul in verses 15–16 tell us about how God works to accomplish his will?
    - From verses 17–19, describe Ananias. What kind of person was he?

6. Enlist someone to read Acts 9:20–22, 26–28 as the group listens for three reactions to Paul's conversion.
    - How did the Jews in the synagogues respond?
    - How did the Christians in Jerusalem receive Paul?
    - What role did Barnabas play in helping Paul find acceptance?

Encourage Application

7. Refer to the *Study Guide* and read the small article, "Conversion Experience." Pose question 1 from the *Study Guide*: "Reflecting on Paul's encounter with Jesus on the Damascus road, what elements of his experience are similar to your personal encounter with Jesus?" Encourage several members to share personal stories of how they came to faith in Christ. Note that Paul told his story often when he was witnessing in front of non-believers—even kings and governors (see Acts 22; 26).

8. State: *Whenever God brings a person to faith in Christ, God has a place for that person to work in his kingdom. Some are leaders like Paul; some are personal witnesses like Ananias; and some are mentors and encouragers like Barnabas.* Challenge members to pray that God will show them their roles in bringing people to Christ, even people they might consider to be unlikely to become Christians.

FOCAL TEXT
Acts 11:1–26

BACKGROUND
Acts 10:1—11:26

MAIN IDEA

Led by God's Spirit, Peter and the church at Antioch crossed high cultural and theological barriers to reach people with the gospel.

QUESTION TO EXPLORE

How can you and your church cross over, break down, or go around barriers that keep you and your church from reaching people different from you with the good news about Jesus?

TEACHING AIM

To lead the class to identify barriers God is challenging you and your church to cross in order to reach all people with the gospel

LESSON NINE

Cross Barriers to Reach Everyone

BIBLE COMMENTS

Understanding the Context

The Book of Acts tells the story of the first-century church and how its humble beginnings gained a foothold in a godless world to become a community of believers spread all across that world. This amazing growth did not happen overnight and not without significant obstacles.

Persecution, natural disasters, famine, and the godless influences of the Roman Empire threatened the church from without. Yet, the most formidable obstacle to confront the early followers of Jesus came from within. Racial and cultural prejudice could have destroyed the growth and influence of the early church. These first-century followers of Jesus had to find a way to overcome the animosity and division between Jew and Gentile.

Providentially, the path of a Gentile named Cornelius crossed with that of Peter, the Jewish fisherman who walked with Jesus. The result was a new understanding of God's ultimate purpose, the salvation of both Jew and Gentile. The events revolving around these two men shed light on how modern followers of Jesus can remove the barriers that keep the church from reaching people with the gospel message.

Interpreting the Scriptures

Acts 11:1–16 is a summary of the events described in Acts 10. Acts 10 recounts the story of Cornelius and Peter.

The Vision of Cornelius (10:1–8)

Cornelius, a Roman centurion who lived in Caesarea, was "one who feared God" (Acts 10:1).[1] This phrase denoted one who was not a full Jewish proselyte but one who believed in God and showed respect for Jewish customs and practices. While at prayer, he had a vision in which he was instructed to send men to Joppa to contact a man named Peter and bring him back to Caesarea.

The Vision of Peter (10:9–23)

The next day, as the representatives of Cornelius approached Joppa (Caesarea was thirty miles north of Joppa), Peter was on the rooftop of his host's house at the time of daily prayers. While a meal was being prepared, Peter had a vision from God. A sheet was lowered from heaven and placed before Peter. On the sheet was an assortment of animals and birds, some considered clean to eat by Jewish regulations and some considered unclean for Jews to eat. When Peter refused to eat, the divine reply "what God has cleansed, no longer consider unholy" (10:15) perplexed Peter, causing him to wonder what the vision meant. Immediately, the friends of Cornelius appeared at the house and entreated the fisherman to come with them back to Caesarea. The hour was late, and so Peter invited these Gentiles into the house and offered them lodging for the night.

Peter and Cornelius (10:24–48)

Peter kept his divine appointment with Cornelius, and the results were miraculous. On arriving, Peter acknowledged his misgivings. Cornelius then recounted his vision in which the angelic messenger instructed him to send for Peter. When Peter realized this Gentile audience waited for any words he would say, the apostle shared with them the gospel, the good news of Jesus the Christ. In the midst of Peter's sharing, the Holy Spirit "fell upon all those who were listening to the message" (10:44). A host of Gentiles were baptized (see 10:24), and Peter stayed with them for several days, encouraging them in their newfound faith.

Committed to Rituals, not Grace (11:1–3)

News spread quickly concerning Peter's encounter with Cornelius. The statement "those who were circumcised took issue with him" refers to Jewish Christians. They were concerned because Peter had associated with Gentiles and ignored dietary restrictions. They showed no joy over the report of the conversion of Cornelius and his friends. This strong commitment to ritual and prejudice over grace and freedom was a recurring issue facing these first believers, and it still sidetracks followers of Jesus today.

The Meaning of Peter's Vision (11:4–10)

Peter responded boldly to the ones who took issue with him concerning the Cornelius encounter.

11:4. Peter was careful to explain his actions "in orderly sequence." The entire episode was not Peter's doing; it was the work of the Holy Spirit. God was behind all the events Cornelius and Peter experienced. Peter would never have taken this initiative on his own. His religious prejudices ran too deep. Cornelius, although a God-fearer, would never have had the influence to persuade a total stranger, who just happened to be one of the Twelve, to come into his home and open the door of salvation for Gentiles.

11:7–8. In recounting the vision he had on the rooftop of Simon the tanner's home, Peter's attitude was so ingrained that he first refused to even consider God's command to "kill and eat" (it was not a request or a suggestion).

11:9–10. The vision and dialogue happened three times. God made sure Peter understood the significance of what was about to unfold. Peter's allegiance to Jewish regulations could have blinded him from seeing the significance of this vision. Providentially, this did not happen. From this point, Peter had his relapses and backed away a bit (Galatians 2:11–14), but he never went into full retreat.

Obeying the Promptings of the Spirit (11:11–14)

Peter emphasized the providential nature of these events as he recounted the arrival of the friends of Cornelius at the house where Peter was staying. When it really mattered, Peter removed any moment of awkwardness with the invitation for these Gentile visitors to come in and stay the night (10:23).

The Spirit instructed Peter to go "without misgivings" with these men to Caesarea. Peter took six Jewish believers with him, no doubt for both support and corroboration.

From Prejudice to Relationship (11:15–17)

11:15–16. What happened to Cornelius, his relatives, and his friends was exactly the same thing that happened to Peter and those who had first gathered when the Holy Spirit came upon them. Peter and his six companions witnessed the same gift given to them, God's Spirit, now given to Gentiles as well.

11:17. "Therefore if God gave to them the same gift as He gave to us also after believing in the Lord Jesus Christ, who was I that I could stand in God's way?" The term translated "stand" is the same word rendered "prevents" when the Ethiopian Gentile asked Philip whether he could be baptized (8:36) as well as the term "refuse" when Peter exclaimed that no one could hinder the people in the house of Cornelius from experiencing baptism (10:47). Here Peter asserted that to deny the conversion and acceptance of these Gentiles was to stand against God himself. Note that baptism occurred after the experience of salvation for Cornelius and his friends. The baptism of *believers only* is biblical.

Barriers Broken (11:18)

"Well then, God has granted to the Gentiles also the repentance that leads to life." Sadly, this response by those who took issue with Peter did not end the matter. As with most public responses, the attitudes were mixed as later events in Acts show (see Acts 15).

A Church on Fire for God (11:19–26)

11:19–21. These verses reveal that persecution fostered the spread of the gospel. The martyrdom of Stephen (6:8—7:60) was followed by the scattering of those believers who remained. They left their homes, jobs, and possessions and "made their way to Phoenicia and Cyprus and Antioch." Phoenicia was a country stretching along the northeastern coast of the Mediterranean Sea. Cyprus was an island in the northeastern Mediterranean. Antioch was known as the third city of the Roman Empire (following Rome and Alexandria). The first congregation that was predominately Gentile was located in this city. Paul's three missionary journeys were also launched from this church.

Those who settled in these areas apparently did not go into hiding or spend much time grieving over their losses. They shared the message of salvation, but did so "speaking the word to no one except to Jews alone" (11:19). But not all restricted their sharing to Jews. Others came to Antioch and engaged Gentiles in discussions concerning Jesus. This effort yielded great success. Many Gentiles accepted Jesus as Savior.

11:22–24. As Peter's experience with Cornelius had caught the attention of the Jewish Christian leaders in Jerusalem ("those who were circumcised," 11:2), so did the spiritual events in Antioch. The "church at Jerusalem" dispatched Barnabas to check on things in Antioch. His report was positive and in the same spirit as Peter's report of events concerning Cornelius and other Gentiles.

11:25–26. The narrative of Acts takes a significant and pivotal turn as Barnabas attempted to locate Saul of Tarsus. The news of the conversion of this dogmatic persecutor of Christians had caused no little disturbance among the people. Barnabas found Saul, persuaded him to return with him to Antioch, and there they stayed for a year. The narrative closes with the mention that "the disciples were first called Christians in Antioch" (11:26). The church at Antioch would play a significant role in bringing the good news of Jesus to all people, to Jews as well as Gentiles.

Focusing on the Meaning

Present-day followers of Jesus can no longer ignore the clear message of Scripture; salvation is God's gift to all people. Although our society has taken significant steps in removing barriers of racial prejudice, we still have much to accomplish. Churches still face barriers that prevent people who need the Lord from ever having the opportunity of choosing to follow Jesus.

Identify the barriers that exist today. Every congregation faces at least one of the following barriers that blunt our effectiveness:

Language barriers. We don't have to let communication barriers keep us from reaching out to one another. We live in a world where language learning is easily accessible. Encourage your church to offer English classes for those who need it, and encourage members to learn how to communicate with the language group.

Cultural barriers. The fact that someone with a different background lives in your neighborhood should be a reminder that God loves and cares for all people. Do you?

Racial prejudice. If this sin keeps you from reaching out to other people, then do the following: Confess this sin and pray for an opportunity to reach out to someone whose skin color is different from yours. Then the next day, repeat this process. You will most likely have to practice this for the rest of your life.

Geographical barriers. Sometimes, we promote sending funds and missionaries to those areas far away from where we live as a way to excuse our own unwillingness to go. Other times, we consider faraway places as *out of sight and out of mind* and not our concern. Both of these attitudes are wrong. Consider the part of town where you live that is no more than perhaps five minutes from your door, but it might as well be on the other side of the globe. What can your church do to break down the geographical barriers that keep you from sharing Jesus with those who are literally just across town?

Economic barriers. Do we have to live in a world where we constantly evaluate people based on *those who have* and *those who do not have*? What would your church look like if all people were welcomed regardless of the size of their wallet?

May God give us visions like those of Peter and Cornelius. What they started, we must continue.

TEACHING PLANS

Teaching Plan—Varied Learning Activities

Connect with Life

1. Begin by asking the group to listen and respond as you read the story in the first paragraph of this lesson, which begins, "This is America. We speak English." Follow the story by dividing listeners into two teams, and assigning one of these topics to each:

(1) Reasons People Object to the Diversity in America Today

(2) Reasons God Includes All People Groups in His Plan of Salvation

(If more than twelve are in attendance, form additional teams with duplicate assignments.) Allow three to five minutes for teams to discuss and list several reasons. Reassemble for each to state their strongest reasons. (Possible answers for Team 1: the cost of social programs; discomfort with other languages and cultures; a desire to be in control. Possible answers for Team 2: all people are of equal value to God; all have sinned and need salvation; God has empowered his church for the task.)

2. After the sharing, acknowledge that diversity can be difficult for most people—even Christians—to handle with grace. Refer to the *Study Guide,* and read the Study Aim and the Question to Explore for this lesson.

Guide Bible Study

3. Have Acts 11:1–3 read as the group listens for the two questions that faced early Jewish Christians. Write their answers as column 1 under, "Diversity in the Early Churches." (1) Could Gentiles become Christians without fully becoming Jews first? (2) Could Jewish Christians participate in fellowship meals with Gentile Christians? Give background from paragraph four in the lesson introduction in the *Study Guide* and from the *Study Guide* section, "Two Big Questions."

4. Ask, *What diversity issues are tearing apart American churches and denominations today that might parallel the concerns of the early churches?* Write answers in column 2, "Diversity Issues Today."

5. As readers follow along in the Acts 11:4–16 narrative, ask someone (who has been enlisted and prepared in advance) to read the italicized words from "Peter's Experience" in the *Study Guide* as a monologue. Afterward call attention to the fact that Luke included the full story twice—first in chapter 10, and repeated in chapter 11.

Inquire why they think he gave that much precious parchment to this incident.

6. Read aloud Acts 11:15–18 as the group listens for the role of the Holy Spirit in the Cornelius event. Call for additional verses to be read in sequence: Acts 10:19–20, 30–31, 44–45. Discuss ways believers can recognize the work of the Holy Spirit in the diversity issues that divide churches today.

7. Call for someone to read Acts 11:19–26 as listeners try to determine why the Antioch church was less questioning of diversity than the Jerusalem church. Find help in the *Study Guide* section, "Continuing to Cross Barriers." Ask, *Which church had a better grasp of Jesus' words in Acts 1:8?*

Encourage Application

8. Play and discuss Ken Medema's song, "What's Going On at Antioch?" (See footnote 9 in the *Study Guide.*) **Alternate idea:** Relate the words of the hymn, "In Christ There Is No East or West," to this study.[2]

9. Refer to the list, "Diversity Issues Today" (Step 4 above), and ask learners to identify issues that most affect your church or association of churches. Plan one action your group could take to make a positive difference toward healing, such as holding a block party with free hot dog supper and a concert of Christian music; or providing Bible study materials for a group that speaks English as a second language (Reference the small articles, "Bible Study Resources in Other Languages" and "Table Fellowship," in the *Study Guide.*)

10. **Alternate idea:** If your group took on the "Philip Project" (see Lesson 7, Step 6) encourage members to tell their experiences. To continue the witnessing momentum, plan an activity to which you can invite the people for whom you have been praying.

Teaching Plan—Lecture and Questions

Connect with Life

1. Ask whether anyone saw the movie or read the book, *The Help,*
   which told the story of our segregated South through the experiences of African American women who worked as domestic help
   for privileged families before the Civil Rights laws were passed.
   Ask, *What causes one race or economic class to treat others with
   prejudice? What barriers were established to keep the help "in their
   place"?*

2. Contrast that with John Grisham's novel, *A Time to Kill,* as refer-
   enced in the *Study Guide* section, "The Big Answer." Affirm that
   Christians can overcome barriers, in the power of God's Spirit.
   Refer to the *Study Guide* and read the Main Idea and the Question
   to Explore.

Guide Bible Study

3. Write on the board the two big questions that faced Jewish
   Christians in the Jerusalem church (see paragraph four in the
   lesson introduction in the *Study Guide*).

   (1) Could Gentiles become Christians without fully becoming
       Jews first?

   (2) Could Jewish and Gentile Christians actually eat a fellowship
       meal together?

4. On a map of Israel in New Testament times, locate key places in
   today's study: (1) Jerusalem—center of church life and authority; (2)
   Caesarea on the Samaria coast—home of Cornelius, a God-fearing
   Roman centurion; and (3) Antioch of Syria—where a new church
   was breaking down old barriers.

5. Summarize briefly the story of Peter and Cornelius, as told in Acts
   10. Then call for a reading of Acts 11:1–3. Ask, *What was the main
   criticism of Peter by the Jerusalem church leaders? Why do you think
   eating with Gentiles was questioned more than the conversion of*

Gentiles? Give further background from the *Study Guide* section, "Two Big Questions."

6. Ask listeners to count the times the Holy Spirit is mentioned in Acts 11:4–16. Write "Holy Spirit" on the board. Verse 5 tells of Peter's vision in which the Lord spoke to him. Write "Vision and Voice" on the board. Verse 13 mentions an angel visitor to Cornelius. Add "angel" to the board. Ask, *Why do you think heaven was so involved in this event at Cornelius's house? Can you believe that God will be as present and powerful when you and your church step out to cross barriers and share the gospel?*

7. Read the victorious outcome in Acts 11:15–18. Point out that this milestone was so important that Luke told the complete story twice: in both Acts 10 and Acts 11. Ask members to list all the barriers that were crossed that day (traditions, prejudices, arrogance, fear, language, and culture, to mention a few).

8. Contrast the Jerusalem and Antioch churches from Acts 11:19–26. (For assistance, see "Continuing to Cross Barriers" in the *Study Guide*.) Probe the passage with these questions:
   - How did the Antioch church get started?
   - What was their *target group* in verse 19?
   - How did their focus expand in verse 20?
   - Did God bless their efforts to reach the Greeks?
   - Why might it have been easier for the Antioch church to cross barriers?
   - How do you see God's hand in the selection of Barnabas to investigate?

Encourage Application

9. Point out that Antioch is where Christ's followers were first dubbed, "Christians." Read question 6 from the questions near the end of the lesson in the *Study Guide* ("If church members weren't already called Christians today, what would people call us?"). Ask, *Why does the term "Christian" sometimes carry negative connotations?*

How can churches and individuals better show that we are "Christ-ones"? What barrier-breaking ministries is our church involved in this year?

NOTES

1. Unless otherwise indicated, all Scripture quotations in lessons 1–3 and 9–11 are taken from the 1995 update of the New American Standard Bible®.
2. Words by John Oxenham, 1852–1941.

FOCAL TEXT
Acts 13:1–5, 13–14, 42–52

BACKGROUND
Acts 13

MAIN IDEA
The church at Antioch unhesitatingly obeyed the Spirit's leading to send missionaries out, and Barnabas and Paul boldly went, proclaiming Jesus to Jews and then to Gentiles.

QUESTIONS TO EXPLORE
How are we doing today in sending and being missionaries? Are you ready to go? to send?

TEACHING AIM
To lead participants to trace how the church at Antioch reached out to the world through the mission work of Barnabas and Paul and to evaluate their own participation in missions, whether sending or going

LESSON TEN
Be Jesus' Witness Beyond Where You Are

BIBLE COMMENTS

Understanding the Context

The best outline of the entire Book of Acts is Acts 1:8: "You will receive power when the Holy Spirit has come upon you; and you shall be My witnesses both in Jerusalem, and in all Judea and Samaria, and even to the remotest part of the earth." Those gathered in the upper room asked God for direction. Their prayers were answered as God led those first believers to begin to take the story of Jesus to any who would listen. Soon the disciples fanned out from Jerusalem, throughout Judea and Samaria, telling the good news.

How did these first followers of Jesus respond to the command to go to the ends of the earth? Did they understand the implications of moving beyond their own country and engaging all people with the gospel? The remaining chapters of the Book of Acts describe how the disciples of Jesus carried out this final phase. This phase is still going on today. As long as people exist who have yet to hear or accept the gospel, then the command to send and to be missionaries must be obeyed.

Acts 13 describes the calling of Barnabas and Saul to leave their familiar surroundings and take the gospel to faraway places. The Holy Spirit clearly called these two men to pack up and move out to unknown regions. This calling took place as Barnabas and Saul were serving the church at Antioch. Present-day followers of Jesus have much to learn from this church. They gladly sent out their best and provided much needed support for this first missionary trip, which would change the course of history.

Interpreting the Scriptures

Leaders in the Church (13:1)

The church at Antioch became the center of operations for the missionary work of Barnabas and Saul. Barnabas, who was known for his generosity and encouraging spirit (Acts 4:36–37), was sent by the leaders of the Jerusalem church to investigate and report back concerning the events that had taken place in Antioch (11:22–26). Saul, known also as Paul (13:9), had spent a year in Antioch teaching the people and developing leaders within the congregation.

They were joined by other leaders in the church. "Simeon, who was called Niger," most likely was a Jewish man from North Africa. "Niger," a term meaning *black,* describes his dark skin. Lucius of Cyrene may identify one who was present on the day of Pentecost who made his way to Antioch with other prophets from this Libyan city (11:20). Manaen was the foster brother of Herod Antipas. These two men, raised in the same atmosphere and given the same opportunities, chose different paths of life. Manaen became a powerful prophet within the early church, while Herod Antipas used his authority to put John the Baptist to death (Luke 9:7–9) and to deny Jesus justice on the night before his crucifixion (Luke 23:7–12).

The Call of the Spirit (13:2–3)

The idea of sending Barnabas and Saul/Paul on a missionary journey was not the result of a planning meeting. The Holy Spirit prompted this gathering of prophets, teachers, and leaders as they worshiped, prayed, and fasted. This *sending out* was witnessed by the congregation. The prophets and teachers prayed, fasted, laid their hands on the two missionaries, and sent them on their way.

A Pattern for Church Planting (13:4–5)

13:4. Leaving Antioch, they traveled to the port city of Seleucia (sixteen miles to the west) and set sail for the island of Cyprus. This island, now in Roman hands, was an important military stronghold as well as a commercial center. When Barnabas and Saul landed there, Sergius Paulus was the appointed governor of the island (13:6–12).

13:5. Salamis, a city on the eastern side of the island, had a large enough Jewish population to warrant more than one synagogue. The missionaries began their work in the synagogues. This pattern of reaching the Jews first became the template for Paul's later ministry. Although he became frustrated with their lack of response and gravitated more toward taking the gospel to Gentiles, Paul never gave up on his desire to win his own people to Christianity.

John, also known as Mark, was the cousin of Barnabas (Colossians 4:10). The account of his deserting the missionaries on this journey, the subsequent falling out between Barnabas and Paul over whether to include this young man in their work, and the reconciliation of Paul and John Mark in later years, is an amazing story of redemption and forgiveness (Acts 15:36–41; 2 Timothy 4:11).

Barnabas and Paul proclaimed the "word of God." This expression appears often in the Acts account (see 4:31; 6:2; 8:14; 11:1; 12:24; 17:13; 18:11). In each of these instances, the context suggests the "word of God" was the telling of the gospel, the story of salvation. The phrase can describe God's will and plan in broad terms, but in the Acts account the use of the phrase pointed to the cross and its implications for those who heard it.

Proclaiming Jesus to Jews (13:13–41)

13:13–14. Sailing from Cyprus, the missionary team arrived in Perga, a city located in the coastal province of Pamphylia. John Mark left them and returned to Jerusalem. Whatever his reason for leaving, Paul's dissatisfaction and loss of confidence in the younger man resulted in a break with Barnabas (15:36–41).

13:15–41. Traveling from Perga to Pisidian Antioch (110 miles to the north) "on the Sabbath day they went into the synagogue and sat down" (13:14). The pattern of beginning their work at the synagogue (13:5) continued when they reached Pisidian Antioch. The synagogue leaders invited Paul and Barnabas to speak to the gathering. Paul then stood and delivered the word of God, a concise summary of Jewish history beginning with the days of Egyptian captivity and proclaiming Jesus as the promised Savior (13:16–41).

Proclaiming Jesus to Gentiles (13:42–52)

13:42–44. Paul's "word of God" message was met with a mixed reaction. Many of the Jews and Gentile "God-fearing proselytes" (13:43) begged Paul and Barnabas to return the next Sabbath in order to continue their teaching. So the next Sabbath, "nearly the whole city assembled to hear the word of the Lord" (13:44).

13:45–47. The reaction of the Jewish leaders was swift and brutal. They felt threatened and began a smear campaign against Paul and Barnabas. The reaction of the missionaries to this attack was equally swift and brutal. Paul and Barnabas felt obligated to speak the word of God to their own people first, but in light of their rejection, the missionaries announced, "we are turning to the Gentiles" (13:46). This statement signaled they were now committed to go beyond what was considered acceptable and normal by Jews and Jewish Christians in relating to Gentiles.

The use of the Old Testament in the New Testament (13:47) is seen in the combining of the words of Isaiah 42:6 and 49:6. These Old Testament prophecies reminded the Jews they were to be witnesses, not just to their own but to the Gentiles as well.

13:48. "When the Gentiles heard this, they began rejoicing and glorifying the word of the Lord; and as many as had been appointed to eternal life believed." Salvation involves both divine initiative and human response.

13:49–52. God's word spread throughout the whole region, no doubt due to the many Gentiles who were welcomed into God's family. Such a positive response brought a plot on the part of the Jews. When opposition did not stop the missionaries, the Jewish leaders convinced other leading citizens that these men were dangerous. They succeeded in driving Paul and Barnabas out of the city. Paul and Barnabas symbolically shook the dust off their shoes as a sign of protest and went to the next town, Iconium. They also left behind many new Christians who were excited and encouraged in the Lord.

Focusing on the Meaning

Missions should be the very heartbeat of our churches. Many congregations are generous with mission giving and have positive responses to local mission projects, but they fall short when it comes to fulfilling the mandate of taking the gospel to the ends of the earth (Acts 1:8).

Present-day churches must continually find ways to follow the pattern set by the New Testament church when they took the gospel beyond their own familiar surroundings.

Consider three ways to continue the pattern found in the mission strategy of the first-century church.

Teach missions. Keep the focus on missions by including it as part of the regular teaching and worshiping emphases of the church. If people do not know the biblical mandate to take the gospel to the ends of the earth, then they will never feel a sense of responsibility or obligation.

Engage in short-term mission trips. Plan trips that will allow people to experience doing mission work away from home. Careful planning will enable groups to minister in a foreign setting, spending only a week away from work and other responsibilities.

Support people who answer the call to go. God still calls individuals and families to relocate to unfamiliar places in order to take the gospel to those in need. The church at Antioch encouraged and supported their missionaries. The congregation was willing to send out their best. The Spirit's call to present-day followers of Jesus is both to *send out* missionaries and to *be* missionaries. Do we hear the Spirit's call?

May God continue to call us to send and to go.

TEACHING PLANS

Teaching Plan—Varied Learning Activities

Connect with Life

1. Prior to class, place four posters throughout your room. Write one of the following on each poster: "Jerusalem: Familiar," "Judea: Nearby," "Samaria: Uncomfortable," and "Remotest Parts of the Earth: Distant." If you have a large class, post more of the same title in the same location for faster turnover. Provide enough pens at each site so that several people can write at once (see step 3).

2. Read Acts 1:8 aloud. Explain the locations listed in the verse represented the following: Jerusalem represented familiar territory; Judea, nearby territory; Samaria, territory where they felt uncomfortable; and the remotest parts of the earth, distant territory.

3. Ask the class to spend ten minutes at as many of these posted sites as they can, writing things the location listed represents in their lives. Examples for Jerusalem might be a small hometown, workplace, or gym.

4. Lead the group in prayer.

Guide Bible Study

5. Read Acts 1:8 again. Note that in Acts 13, early missionaries followed Jesus' instructions, moving from the familiar to the remotest parts of the earth as they witnessed.

6. Ask, *What does it mean to witness something? What does it means to be Jesus' witness? How are you Jesus' witness?*

7. Enlist someone to read Acts 13:1–5. Then refer to the section in the *Study Guide* titled "God Always Has a Plan." Summarize the comments about the church. Note that not only Saul and Barnabas responded with a *yes* to the Holy Spirit, but the church did as well when they sent out the missionaries. End by referring to their first stop, Cyprus, a familiar place to Barnabas, who was from there. They also first reached out to Jews, which would also have been familiar.

8. Have someone read Acts 13:13–14; 42–45. Then refer to the section in the *Study Guide* titled "Commitment, Theology, and Common Sense." Highlight the locations visited by the missionaries. Note that Paul now reached out to both Jews and Gentiles. Remind your class that we are to go to uncomfortable places. Ask, *What were some uncomfortable things for these missionaries?*

9. Invite someone to read Acts 13:46–52. Then refer to the section in the *Study Guide* titled "Crossing Barriers with the Gospel Message." Remind the class that the last section showed the message going beyond the Jews in the synagogue to the Gentiles in the

marketplace. Note key points from the current section, but specifically mention that as the Gentiles spread throughout the earth, the gospel did too. Read aloud verse 47.

10. Summarize the section, "Our Response." Ask, *What do we do to share the gospel? to send others to share the gospel? What more is God's Spirit calling us to do, even beyond our comfort zones?*

Encourage Application

11. From groups of six or fewer people. Give a blank sheet of paper to each group and ask them to write the following terms on it, but leave space by each one:

    a. Missionary

    b. Mission Field

    c. Mission Work

    (A copy of the assignment is provided in "Teaching Resource Items" for this study at www.baptistwaypress.org.)

12. Give the groups a few minutes to come up with definitions for each term. Invite the groups to share some of these with the entire class while they remain in their groups.

13. Lead the groups to continue to work together by asking them to think about the beginning exercise (see step 1). Ask them to consider those answers and their group definitions in steps 11–12. Have them write "My Jerusalem," "My Judea," "My Samaria," and "My remotest parts of the earth," on the reverse of the paper. Next to each location, ask them to write either how they have gone to each of these sites or how they have sent someone to each of these sites. Then ask them to write how they can go or how they can send someone to each site in the future.

14. Read Acts 1:8 aloud. Challenge the class to start acting on going, sending, or both to their Jerusalem, Judea, Samaria, and remotest parts of the earth.

15. Close with prayer.

Teaching Plan—Lecture and Questions

Connect with Life

1. Prior to class, post the ways in which your church sends out missionaries. If you need direction in this, contact your church staff. Also, post names of groups within your church that are active in local and distant mission work.

2. Prior to class, create and copy a worksheet for each member that has four equal columns with the headings, "My Jerusalem," "My Judea," "My Samaria," and "My Remotest Parts of the Earth." Distribute the sheets. (A copy of the worksheet is available in "Teaching Resource Items" for this study at www.baptistwaypress.org.)

3. Read Acts 1:8 while the class listens for the locations to which Jesus sent his disciples as missionaries. Point out that this lesson from Acts 13 shows the earliest missionaries acting on the command from this verse. Suggest that to the early church, Jerusalem was an example of familiar territory, Judea stood for nearby territory, Samaria equated to uncomfortable territory, and the remotest parts of the earth meant distant territory.

4. Give examples of what each of those represents for you. For example, your Jerusalem might be your work place, and your Samaria might be serving at a homeless shelter. Ask the class where their Jerusalem, Judea, Samaria, and remotest parts of the earth are. Have them write their answers on their worksheet. Invite comments.

5. Open in prayer.

Guide Bible Study

6. Enlist someone to read Acts 13:1–5. Summarize the section, "God Always has a Plan," in the *Study Guide.* Explain these verses further by using information in "Bible Comments" in this *Teaching Guide.* Specifically talk about the sending out of Barnabas and Paul. From the Questions section in the *Study Guide,* ask question 4, "What

are some concrete examples of (our) church's personal investment in the mission of God?"

7. Refer to and read the small article, "Our Church and Missions," in the *Study Guide*. Ask members to consider how their church is either going themselves or sending others, whether in familiar surroundings (Jerusalem) or to the remotest parts of the earth.

8. Invite someone to read Act 13:13–14, 42–45. Summarize the *Study Guide* section, "Commitment, Theology, and Common Sense," pointing out that these missionaries were in the process of fulfilling Acts 1:8. Explain further as seems helpful using information on these verses in "Bible Comments" in this *Teaching Guide*. Call for a few brief testimonies on mission work from members of your class.

9. Have someone read Acts 13:46–52. Summarize "Crossing Barriers with the Gospel Message." Enlist someone to read verse 52 again, and then ask why they think these men were filled with joy.

10. Summarize the final section in the *Study Guide*, "Our Response," and "Focusing on the Meaning" in this *Teaching Guide*.

Encourage Application

11. Ask:
    a. If you were planning a send-off event for someone leaving to serve in mission work, what activities would you include?
    b. From the Questions section in the *Study Guide*, ask, "How would you describe your personal responsibility in the mission of God?"
    c. Have you ever felt called to mission work? What was your response?
    d. At this point in your life, are you going, sending, both, or neither?

12. Challenge your class to consider their mission fields based on their worksheets from step 2 in this Teaching Plan. Ask, *What can you do now to go or to send? Be as specific as possible.* Ask them to write specific things they could do by either going or sending in each of

these locations. Challenge them to take action on what they have written and talked about in class.

13. Close in prayer.

MAIN IDEA

The church decided that they must focus on Jesus and his grace rather than on non-essential human requirements about salvation and relating to people.

QUESTION TO EXPLORE

What non-essential matters do we allow, whether by custom or conviction, to get in the way of focusing on Jesus and his grace?

TEACHING AIM

To lead the class to summarize the concerns and conclusions of the Jerusalem council and to decide on ways to focus on Jesus and his grace rather than on non-essential human requirements about salvation and relating to people

LESSON ELEVEN
Keep Focused On What's Essential

BIBLE COMMENTS

Understanding the Context

A simple quotation sums up the issue found in Acts 15: "In essentials, unity. In nonessentials, liberty. In all things, charity [love]."[1]

The early church faced a crisis that threatened the very nature of the gospel itself. Since Jesus had ascended to heaven and left his followers with the command to take the message of salvation to the ends of the earth, the first-century church had grown from a small gathering in Jerusalem to a movement that had spread far beyond the borders of Israel. Not only had the gospel reached foreign lands, but it had reached the ears and hearts of Gentiles as well.

Paul and Barnabas returned from their first journey with glowing reports of many Gentiles who had accepted the gift of grace. The crisis centered on how Gentiles were to be welcomed in the community of faith. Would they be compelled to become Jews first, keeping the requirements of the Jewish law? Was salvation found in accepting Jesus as Savior alone or were other strings and conditions attached?

Interpreting the Scriptures

Division (15:1–5)

15:1. The issue was clear to some. Gentiles must accept Christ *and* become practicing followers of Judaism in order to be saved. The rite of circumcision was the litmus test, but submission to all the minute details of the Jewish legalistic system was included as well. Many commentators label these men from Judea who came to Antioch as *Judaizers*.

15:2–5. Paul and Barnabas realized the serious nature of this perversion of the gospel and did not sit back and watch. Instead, they vigorously debated and refuted the teaching of these Judaizers, who mixed law and grace in a tragic combination.

The leaders of the church at Antioch sent Paul and Barnabas to Jerusalem to confer with the leaders there in order to seek a resolution regarding this issue. One should not underestimate the seriousness of this section of the Book of Acts. Paul and Barnabas had just returned from a very successful mission trip where many Gentiles responded to the gospel. But now Judaizers were seeking to change the very message they preached. Persecution from outside the community could be endured, but attacks and undermining from within could derail the mission of the early church.

When Paul and Barnabas arrived in Jerusalem, the lines were drawn. On one side were those who believed as these two missionaries that salvation was intended for both Jew and Gentile on the basis of faith in Christ alone. On the other side were those who demanded Gentiles also accept and practice the laws of Judaism in order to be welcomed into the household of faith.

Debate (15:6–18)

Peter spoke concerning what he had experienced in past days (Acts 15:6–11). Barnabas and Paul shared about their experiences in the present time (15:12). James concluded the debate by focusing on what this issue meant for the future work of the churches.

15:6–11. Peter was a respected leader within the Jerusalem church. No one could question his loyalty to Judaism. His view could sway the decision one way or the other.

Peter not only believed Gentiles should be welcomed into the church without the burden of legalism, but the apostle also asserted that God's plan included "that by my mouth the Gentiles would hear the word of the gospel and believe" (15:7). He was no bystander regarding this issue. He had firsthand knowledge of how God was at work among the Gentiles. He underscored his view a second time, asserting that God "made no distinction between us and them, cleansing their hearts by faith" (15:9). Then a third time he stated: "But we believe that we are saved through the grace of the Lord Jesus, in the same way as they also are" (15:11). Peter spoke forcefully. His view concerning the salvation of Gentiles could not be misunderstood. Salvation was by grace through faith alone, with nothing added. No doubt his thoughts centered on his experience with Cornelius several years before (10:1—11:18; see lesson 9).

15:12. Barnabas and Paul related the success of their recent journey, which included stops on the island of Cyprus and in the communities in Asia Minor. What Peter experienced in the past, they were experiencing in the present. God was at work as Barnabas and Paul took the gospel to Gentiles.

15:13–18. James, the brother of Jesus, concluded the debate by speaking of the future implications of bringing the gospel to both Jews and Gentiles. James appealed to the Old Testament prophecy found in Amos 9:11–12. This passage anticipates Gentiles becoming part of God's kingdom when the house of David is restored. James interpreted this restoration in light of the coming of Jesus the Messiah. Therefore Gentiles come into the family of God, not by becoming Jews, but by putting their faith in Jesus. From this point on, both Jew and Gentile would experience salvation in the same way. The ground at the foot of the cross was now level for all who would come to Jesus for salvation.

Decision (15:19–29)

15:19. James clearly sided with Peter, Barnabas, and Paul. He suggested a compromise. Jewish believers would not frustrate or "trouble" Gentiles concerning salvation by faith. In return, Gentiles would agree to avoid certain things so as not to frustrate and offend Jews.

15:20. The fourfold list was proposed to help Gentiles turn away from idolatry. These new converts needed to make a clean break from their past in order to live faithful lives. Things contaminated by idols referred to food that had been offered as a sacrifice to a pagan god. Gentiles were to turn away from anything and everything involved in idol worship.

Pagan temples throughout the Roman world included sexual immorality in their practices. Temple prostitutes received offerings from worshipers and in return offered their bodies as an act of worship to the gods. One could not love Jesus and participate in such immoral practices.

Gentiles were admonished not to eat the meat of strangled animals as well as any animal whose blood had not been drained. Perhaps Leviticus 17:10–16 provided the reasoning for the issue concerning blood, but neither this passage nor any other passage in the Old Testament mentions the meat of a strangled animal. This practice was familiar to those living in the first century, though, because strangled animals were believed to appease demonic spirits as part of idol worship.

15:21. "For Moses from ancient generations has in every city those who preach him, since he is read in the synagogues every Sabbath." This concluding statement of James was a solemn reminder that this issue was far from settled. Although the Jerusalem Council had agreed to receive Gentile converts on the basis of faith and although they had authored a set of guidelines to help Gentiles turn away from idolatry, there would always be those who would seek to coerce Gentiles into adopting legalism as part of their commitment to Jesus. James could not have spoken truer words.

Some commentators equate this conference (Acts 15) with the meeting Paul described in Galatians 2:1–10. Other scholars equate Galatians 2 with the visit to Jerusalem described in Acts 11:30. If this latter view be the case, then the dissension concerning Gentile converts had been raised long before the Jerusalem conference of Acts 15.

15:22–29. Those present at the council in Jerusalem drafted a letter for Paul and Barnabas along with two leaders from the Jerusalem church, Judas Barsabbas and Silas, to deliver to the leaders of the church in Antioch. This letter stated that Gentiles would be received into the family of faith on the basis of faith alone, with no requirement of circumcision. The letter further outlined the four guidelines intended to help Gentile converts break away from the practice of idol worship.

Focusing on the Meaning

Just as idolatry is alive and well in our world today, so is legalism. Consider where you and your church are in relation to the quotation mentioned at the beginning of this lesson.

"In essentials, unity." We should all agree on the basic issues of our faith, such as that God created all things, Jesus Christ is Lord, the Bible is God's word, and salvation is a gift of grace received by faith. These basic beliefs draw people together and promote unity and fellowship.

"In nonessentials, liberty." This is where tension exists for many Christians. Have you ever heard the following nonessential things

elevated to the level of mandatory requirements? *You are not welcome in my church if you do not dress like I do. You are not welcome in my church if your children are not perfect. You are not welcome in my church if you don't cut your hair. You are not welcome in my church if you have a tattoo. When the music in the worship service is like I want it, I'll be back.*

Now imagine you are a person who has recently experienced the joy of forgiveness and salvation in Christ. You walk into the church that makes such requirements and quickly find out what that church is all about. How do you feel concerning your spiritual life now?

"In all things, charity [love]." The leaders of the first-century church had their disagreements and heated debates. When all was said and done, they found common ground and determined to do all things in love. They stood together on the essentials, extended freedom to one another on the nonessentials, and spoke and acted out of love for God and one another in all things.

Gentiles were waiting at the door of faith, wanting to come in. Lost people in our day are waiting at this door and wanting to come in as well.

TEACHING PLANS

Teaching Plan—Varied Learning Activities

Connect with Life

1. Prior to class, post the statement, "Name all the ways a person can get into heaven." Read Acts 15:1 to your class. Pointing to the written statement, ask the class to begin giving answers. When they conclude there is only one way, explain that today's lesson talks about a disagreement between early church members. Some believed that faith in Christ was sufficient for salvation. Others believed salvation would occur only when a person trusted in Jesus and lived by Jewish tradition and law.

2. From Questions at the end of the lesson in the *Study Guide,* ask questions 3 and 4, "Do you think people want to add to the requirements of salvation even today? What are some of the elements they want to add?"

3. Open in prayer.

Guide Bible Study

4. Divide the class into four groups (six or fewer people each). Assign each group one of the following sections from the lesson in the *Study Guide*: "The Conflict" (Acts 15:1–5)"; "The Conversation (Acts 15:6–12)"; "The Conclusion (Acts 15:13–21)"; "The Communication (Acts 15:22–29)." Have each group read its section and verses and then prepare a summary of their assigned readings for presentation to the class. To present the summary, choose a member or members from the group to act as one or more main characters from each Scripture passage. Use at least one of the following characters for the listed section:

   a. "The Conflict," Use "some of the sect of the Pharisees" plus Paul and/or Barnabas

   b. "The Conversation," Peter

   c. "The Conclusion," James

   d. "The Communication," Judas (called Barsabbas) and/or Silas

   If you want to add characters to the above listed names, do so, of course. Have the main characters introduce themselves to the class before giving their summary. (A copy of the group instructions is available in "Teaching Resource Items" for this study at www.baptistwaypress.org.)

5. After the last group finishes, ask the class to turn to the final section of the lesson in the *Study Guide,* "Implications and Actions." Summarize this section.

6. Call for thoughts on what the class has heard. Ask, *How would you have handled the situation if you had been part of the early church? Would you have stayed silent? If you think you would have done*

something, what steps would you have taken to keep the focus on Jesus' grace rather than on non-essential elements of salvation?

Encourage Application

7. Read aloud or enlist someone to read aloud the beginning story in the *Study Guide* about the couple who came to church and then left because someone pointed out that coffee was not allowed in the sanctuary. Lead the class to work together in pairs. One person will act in the role of the person who noticed the missing couple. The other person will act in the role of the person who pointed out that drinks were not allowed. Ask the partners to talk about what happened with the couple. Ask, *If you were the person who showed the couple their seats and then noticed they left, how would you feel when you discovered why they left? What would you say to the person when you found out why?* Time permitting, invite the pairs to share their conversation with the class.

8. Ask the class for their thoughts on why people might focus on regulations rather than relationships.

9. Now ask the class to come up with a list of ways they can avoid creating non-essential requirements for salvation. Challenge the class to:

    a. Become aware of their attitudes that might cause some people to turn away from church

    b. Help create situations where all feel welcome

    c. Focus on Christ and his grace rather than strict laws

10. Close in prayer.

Teaching Plan—Lecture and Questions

Connect with Life

1. Invite someone to read or summarize the story in the *Study Guide* about the couple with coffee leaving the church service. Lead the

class to answer the questions posed in paragraph three of that section. Now lead your class through the case study in the *Study Guide* about this incident.

2. Prior to class, post the question from the lesson's Question to Explore, "What non-essential matters do we allow, whether by custom or conviction, to get in the way of focusing on Jesus and his grace?" Call for responses to this question. Not only ask the "what" on this matter, however, but also ask "why" as a church body we might focus on things other than Jesus and his grace.

3. Open in prayer.

Guide Bible Study

4. Read or ask someone to read Acts 15:1–5. Explain 15:1 by referring to 15:5 about "the sect of the Pharisees." Refer also to the information in paragraph two in the *Study Guide* under "The Conflict (15:1–5)." Explain 15:1–5 using information in "The Conflict" and in "Bible Comments" on these verses in this *Teaching Guide*. Ask, *What are some things that divide churches today?* (Examples: the type of music played, an unspoken dress code.)

5. Read or ask someone to read Acts 15:6–12. Explain these verses using information under the heading, "The Conversation (15:6–12)," and in "Bible Comments" on these verses in this *Teaching Guide*. Read verses 8–11 again. Call for thoughts on these verses. Ask, *How do you think these verses might apply to church conflicts and divisions today?*

6. Read or ask someone to read Acts 15:13–21. Explain these verses using information under "The Conclusion (15:13–21)" and in "Bible Comments" on these verses in this *Teaching Guide*. Point out that two issues were at stake: one, the matter of adding actions, such as circumcision, to reach salvation; two, the matter of the Jews and Gentiles having conflict because of tradition. Emphasize that when the Jerusalem council concluded there were actions the Gentiles should abstain from, it was not about adding non-essential requirements to salvation. Rather it was about strengthening the relationship between the two cultures.

7. Read or ask someone to read Acts 15:22–29. Talk about the main points of the section, "The Communication." Finish by highlighting points from the final section of the lesson, "Implications and Actions."

Encourage Application

8. Ask questions 3, 4, and 5 in the *Study Guide* to summarize and apply the lesson.

9. Challenge the class to focus on the sufficiency of Jesus' grace rather than adding things that God does not require for salvation. Refer to and summarize "Focusing on the Meaning" for this lesson in this *Teaching Guide.*

10. Close in prayer.

NOTES ─────────────────────────────

1. The familiar saying is attributed to various people in Christian history but has been traced to the early seventeenth-century.
See http://www9.georgetown.edu/faculty/jod/augustine/quote.html. Accessed 5/1/2012.

LESSON TWELVE

Witness in Diverse Ways to Diverse People

BIBLE COMMENTS

Understanding the Context

"Keep the main thing the main thing." That plaque in Dr. Roy Fish's seminary office caught my eye when he was my professor and I was visiting him in his office. Given Dr. Fish's teaching area (evangelism) and his commitment to *gossip the gospel in season and out of season,* I had little doubt regarding the sign's meaning.

Whatever else occurred at the Jerusalem Conference, the subject of lesson eleven (see Acts 15:1–29; see also Galatians 2:1–10), at that meeting the early church leaders concluded that *the ground is level at the foot of the cross.* Stated otherwise, they determined that the gospel was for all people, not only for Jews but also for Greeks (note Romans 1:16). What is more, those gathered—including Peter, Paul, and James—decided with the aid of the Holy Scriptures and the Holy Spirit not to require Gentiles to become Jews (that is, to be circumcised) in order to become Christians. They chose to "keep the main thing the main thing."

On the heels of the Jerusalem Council, Paul and Barnabas, who were partners on the so-called first missionary journey (see Acts 13:1—14:28), parted ways over John Mark (15:39). Barnabas took Mark with him to Cyprus, whereas Paul selected Silas to travel with him through Syria and Cilicia (15:40–41). The present lesson begins with Paul, Silas, and Timothy (see 16:1–5) fully engaged in what is now known as the second missionary journey (note 15:36—18:22). More specifically, in this study we will join Paul (and Silas) at three junctures on their Grecian journey—a prison in Philippi (16:25–34), a synagogue in Thessalonica (17:1–4), and the Areopagus in Athens (17:16–33).

Interpreting the Scriptures

Praising God in a Philippian Prison (16:25–34)

16:6–13. A vision that Paul received in Troas (16:9) led him and his ministry colleagues to travel westward to Greece. While other believers had already preached the gospel in what we call Europe (see especially the places listed in Acts 2:8–11), it appears this was the farthest west Paul had yet traveled. Having set sail from Troas, the missioners arrived in Neapolis via the island of Samothrace (16:11). From there, they continued some ten miles inland to Philippi, "a leading city of the district of Macedonia, a Roman colony" (16:12).[1]

16:14–24. Their initial ministry in Philippi was fruitful, resulting in the baptism of Lydia and her household (16:15). Trouble arose, though, when Paul cast a "spirit of divination" (literally a *spirit of the Python,* originally associated with the Delphic oracle in ancient Greece[2]) out of a slave-girl (16:16, 18). This girl's masters were none too pleased with Paul (and Silas) as they watched their hoped-for profits go down the proverbial drain (16:19). They, in turn, had the ministry team "beaten with rods" (see 2 Corinthians 11:25) and thrown into the inner prison, fastening their feet in stocks.

16:25–27. At this point, the plot thickens even as the suspense heightens. In the middle of the night as the imprisoned Paul and Silas were "praying and singing hymns to God" (16:25), an earthquake occurred (16:25–26). This seismic shift shook the prison's foundations, opened its door, and unfastened the prisoners' chains (16:26). Stirred from his slumber, the jailer saw the prison doors opened and presumed that the inmates had fled. The jailer's knee-jerk reaction was to draw his dagger and get ready to take his life. Better to be dead, he figured, than to face the fall-out of escaped prisoners. He was reckoning that he would be the fall guy!

16:28–34. At this point Paul intervened, assuring the jailer that the prisoners were still in place—a miracle in and of itself (16:28)! The jailer, in turn, found his way to Paul and Silas and fell before them with fear and trembling (16:29). Then, having taken them outside of the prison, he put to them the question: "Sirs, what must I do in order that I might be saved?" (author's translation). This question is deliciously ambiguous. *If* the jailer was seeking advice regarding his *physical* safety, the pair parsed his question along decidedly *spiritual* lines. They declared, "Believe in the Lord Jesus, and you will be saved, you and your household" (16:31). In short, he did, and they were (16:34).

Proclaiming Christ in a Thessalonian Synagogue (17:1–4)

16:35—17:1a. Following the conversion and baptism of the Philippian jailer and his household, which would likely have included his wife and children as well as other relatives and slaves, the chief magistrates (Greek, *stratēgoi*) begged Paul and Silas to leave their fair city (16:39). After securing what amounted to an apology for the unjust treatment they had received under the magistrates' administration and after bidding Lydia and other Philippian Christ-followers farewell (16:40), the missionary band traveled southwesterly some 100 miles to the seaport city of Thessalonica.

17:1b–2a. On arrival in Thessalonica, Paul, according to his custom, made connections with a Jewish synagogue (17:1b–2a; see 13:5, 14; 14:1; 17:10, 17; 18:4; 19:8; see also Luke 4:16). Paul's upbringing and learning in Judaism was nothing short of impressive (Galatians 1:14; Philippians 3:4b–6; see Acts 22:3–5; 26:4–5). When possible, Paul would seek to gain entry into a synagogue in order to explain the Scriptures and in so doing proclaim the gospel. In Philippi, there was a "place of prayer" (*proseuchē*), seemingly distinguishable from a synagogue, where (Jewish) women gathered by a river (16:13, 16). In Thessalonica, Acts reports, "there was a synagogue of the Jews."

17:2b–4. Luke, traditionally regarded to be the author of Acts, reports that on three (consecutive) Sabbaths Paul went to the synagogue gathering in Thessalonica and reasoned "with them from the Scriptures." According to 17:3, this reasoning entailed "explaining and proving that it was necessary for the Messiah to suffer and to rise from the dead." Would that we knew the Scriptures to which Paul appealed as he proclaimed Jesus as the crucified, risen Messiah! (See 1 Corinthians 15:3–4; possible texts include Psalm 69:9; Isaiah 53:4–12; Hosea 6:2; Jonah 1:17.) What was the effect of Paul's proclamation? Acts indicates "some [Jews] were persuaded and joined Paul and Silas, along with a great many of the God-fearing Greeks and not a few of the leading women."

17:5–15. If a number of the synagogue worshipers embraced Paul's preaching, other self-respecting synagogue members rejected both the message and the messengers. Indeed, certain Thessalonian Jews "set the city in an uproar," which resulted in the expulsion of Paul and Silas not only from the synagogue but also from the city (Acts 17:5–9). Given the tenuous situation in Thessalonica, where Paul, Silas, Jason, and unnamed others were in essence accused of sedition against the Roman state, "that very night" Thessalonian believers "sent Paul and Silas off to Beroea" (17:10a). In Beroea, a city that lay roughly forty-five miles west of Thessalonica, there was also a Jewish synagogue (17:10b). Acts describes Berean Jews as "more receptive than those in Thessalonica, for they welcomed the message very eagerly and examined the scriptures every day to see whether these things were so" (17:11). Despite the fact that not a few Berean Jews and Greeks believed, Paul was forced to leave the city when certain Thessalonian Jews arrived in the city to make trouble for him (17:12–13). Leaving Silas and Timothy behind in Beroea, Paul journeyed to Athens (17:14–15). It is there we will continue and conclude our lesson.

Presenting the Gospel Before the Athenian Areopagus (17:16–33)

17:16–21. Once in Athens, Paul was "deeply distressed to see that the city was full of idols" (17:16). Instead of withdrawing and heaping scorn on Athens as a cesspool of godless pagans, however, Paul engaged Jews and God-fearers in the synagogue as well as people in the marketplace, including Epicurean and Stoic philosophers. (Whereas Epicureans argued against divine judgment and fear of death, Stoics promoted reason and self-control as essential to living in accord with nature, ruled by the divine *Logos*). The philosophers' curiosity regarding Paul's proclamation of "Jesus and the resurrection" resulted in an opportunity for Paul to address the Areopagus, seemingly an administrative council who derived its name from the Hill of Ares (also known as Mars Hill). (Ares was the Greek god of war to whom the Roman god Mars was roughly equivalent.)

17:22–31. Once in the midst of the Areopagus, Paul acknowledged Athenian religiosity and posited that what they were worshiping as "unknown" was none other than the "God who made the world and everything in it" (17:24). This God, Paul propounded, "does not dwell in temples made with hands . . . neither is he served by human hands . . . " (17:24–25). This God, who from Adam forward made people to search and even grope for him, is close to hand. Indeed, poets like Epimenides ("In him we live . . . ") and Aratus ("We too are his offspring") also recognized God as the ground and source of our being (17:26–28). Given that we are God's "offspring," Paul reasoned, "we ought not to think that the Divine Nature is like gold or silver or stone, an image formed by the art and thought of man" (17:29, NASB). Moreover, given that God has now "appointed" a Man, whom he raised from the dead and through whom he "will judge the world in righteousness," it is now time for all people in all places to repent (17:30–31, NASB).

17:32–34. The Areopagus's response to Paul's proclamation was mixed. Some sneered at the idea of resurrection, while others were willing to ponder the matter further. Still, a few, two of whom Acts mentions by name (Dionysius and Damaris), joined Paul and believed.

Focusing on the Meaning

In 1 Corinthians 9:22, Paul declared, "I have become all things to all people, that I might by all means save [that is, *lead people to a saving faith*] some." This lesson demonstrates Paul's concrete commitment to this considerable claim. When in Philippi, he proclaimed the word to Lydia and other women by the river as well as to the Philippian jailor and his household. When in Thessalonica and Beroea, he sought to persuade synagogue worshipers about the Christ from the Scriptures. Then, in Athens, when addressing the Areopagus, he maintained that the "unknown god" could now be known by means of repentance and belief in the resurrected Jesus.

Ours is a day of spiritual hunger. To fill our God-shaped voids, we, too, have hewn temples for our gods and have fashioned idols for ourselves. Our packaging may differ from the gods worshiped in first-century Athens, but it is no less empty and idolatrous. Even the more noble among us stand in need of the gospel as God calls all people to repent as all are sinful. As we consider our own Philippis, Thessalonicas, Beroeas, and Athenses, may we redouble our commitment to bear winsome witness to the gospel with our lives and our lips. This, no doubt, will require of us uncommon compassion, thoughtful creativity, and determined commitment. When we faithfully, intentionally, and ably share and live the gospel, we model Paul and the Lord he knew and loved so well, and we "keep the main thing the main thing."

TEACHING PLANS

Teaching Plan—Varied Learning Activities

Connect with Life

1. As class members begin to arrive, direct their attention to the following statements written on a poster or whiteboard: "You are opening a brand-new restaurant in town in two weeks. What information does the public need to know?"

2. Lead the class to describe methods that would be best suited to reach the general public (such as television, internet, radio, handbills). Poll the class to answer: (1) which method would be most likely to influence their decisions whether or not to try the restaurant and (2) why that method would most likely be successful.

3. Have a class member read the Main Idea for the lesson from the *Study Guide*. Inform the class that the lesson is a challenge to learn diverse methods of sharing the gospel in their lives. Lead the class in prayer.

Guide Bible Study

4. Quickly review Acts 15 (lesson 11), and summarize Acts 16:1–24. Explain why Paul and Silas were in jail.

5. Read Acts 16:25—34 aloud (or have two students do so). Using the information on these verses in this *Teaching Guide,* explain the jailer's question (16:30) and Paul's response (16:31). Ask:
    • What do you think was the jailer's motivation in asking this question?
    • What do you think is meant by Paul's response? How does this line up with other parts of Scripture relating to salvation? (See, for example, Rom. 10:14–17.)
    • How would you describe the jailer's spiritual awareness before the earthquake? after?

6. Have a learner read 17:1–4. Ask learners to compare Paul's method in this section with the previous section.
   - Why was it Paul's custom to go into the synagogue? (See Rom. 1:16; Matt. 10:5–6.)
   - What did Paul do in the synagogue as he began to speak the gospel? Give learners a few moments to discuss, and then explain Paul's foundation for his discussions in the synagogue (the Scriptures).
   - How was this method suited for the circumstance? (The people in the synagogue were familiar with and committed to the Scriptures.)

7. Summarize 17:5–15. Then enlist someone to read 17:16–21 and someone else to read 17:22–33 aloud. Ask: *How did Paul's approach at Thessalonica and Beroea differ from his approach in Athens?* (He tailored the message to their needs and experiences.) *What was the same?* (He proclaimed the gospel about Jesus.)

8. Utilizing Acts 17:22–32 and the small article titled "Aeropagus" in the *Study Guide,* lead learners to discover the method that Paul used to speak to the philosophers. Ask:
   - Why do you think Paul chose to use this method?
   - How effective was it?
   - What would be an example of such a method today?

Encourage Application

9. Remind learners of the week's Question to Explore in the *Study Guide.* Ask, *What can this passage teach us about sharing the gospel?* Lead the class in discussion of how contextualization can bene-fit Christians when sharing the gospel. Lead learners to describe methods they have used or experienced. (Note: Be sensitive to the possibility that some learners might not be fully committed follow-ers of Christ.)

10. Have a learner read the "Case Study" in the *Study Guide.* Then ask the following questions:
    - Which one of Paul's methods discussed today would be helpful in this situation? Why?

- Is there a different method of expressing the gospel that would be better in this situation?
- If you were the father of the family, is there an approach that you feel would be suited for further discussion?

11. Remind learners that Paul was successful not because of any conversions that occurred, but because of his willingness to share the gospel in diverse settings. Have learners identify one area of their life in which they have expressed hesitancy in sharing the gospel.

12. Close the lesson in prayer, asking God to grant learners wisdom and courage to know when and how to share the gospel.

Teaching Plan—Lecture and Questions

Connect with Life

1. Inform the learners of the Main Idea for the week's lesson. Explain that the purpose of the lesson is to challenge believers today to greater commitment in sharing the gospel in diverse ways. Lead the class in a prayer, asking the Holy Spirit to show areas in which each person can deepen his or her commitment to Christ and openness to sharing the gospel.

Guide Bible Study

2. Quickly review Acts 15 (lesson 11) and summarize Acts 16:1–24. Explain why Paul and Silas were in jail.

3. Read Acts 16:25–34 aloud, and then ask:
   - Why do you think that the jailer was seeking "to be saved"? How sincere do you think he was?
   - What was Paul's response to the jailer?

4. Using the information on Acts 16:30–31 in this *Teaching Guide,* explain the jailer's question (16:30) and Paul's response (16:31). Explain the background of the jailer's "household" to the class using information in this *Teaching Guide* on Acts 16:35.

5. Enlist someone to read 17:1–4 aloud. Explain Paul's use of the Scriptures to communicate the gospel. Ask, *Why did Paul choose to use the Scriptures in contrast to his method with the jailor?* Remind learners that people have different backgrounds for hearing the gospel message. Some people are ready to hear the message of salvation because of their personal needs but have no background in the Scriptures.

6. Summarize 17:5–15. Then call for someone to read 17:16–33 aloud. Direct learners to listen for the number of groups to whom Paul spoke as you read. Ask the following questions:
   - Why would Paul use the method of opening the Scriptures to the people in the synagogue?
   - How was Paul able to use this method?
   - How is it possible that we can use this method today?

7. Using the small article titled "Areopagus" in the *Study Guide,* explain the importance of being able to use the *context* of the listening group to determine the method of speaking to them. Summarize the information under the heading "The Context of the Method" in the *Study Guide.* Ask, *How does contextualization benefit the listener when one presents the gospel?* Guide discussion to include Paul's confession of his methodology in 1 Corinthians 9:19–23.

Encourage Application

8. Say, *In our cultural situation today, churches and individual believers are faced with trying to share the gospel with people who do not automatically share our belief in the authority of Scripture.* Continue with these sentences from the *Study Guide*: "Churches have to be prepared to meet people where they are and to earn the right to witness. Our generation does not have the automatic entrée into people's lives as previous generations did."

9. Ask, *If you were given three minutes to share the gospel, what would you say to*
   - a group of college students
   - a person who is not sure about the existence of God

- a person who laughed as he or she saw you reading your Bible

10. Remind learners that Paul was successful because he was willing to present the gospel in a variety of ways to a variety of listeners. Close the class in prayer, asking God to reveal to them areas in which they can grow to be better prepared to share the gospel in a variety of ways.

NOTES

1. Unless otherwise indicated, all Scripture quotations in lesson 4–6 and 12–13 are from the New Revised Standard Version Bible.

2. See http://www.pbs.org/empires/thegreeks/background/7_p1.html. Accessed 4/25/12.

FOCAL TEXT
Acts 28:17–31

BACKGROUND
Acts 21:17—28:31

MAIN IDEA
The conclusion of the Book of Acts tells of Paul turning to the Gentiles and sharing the gospel without hindrance in the capital city of the Roman Empire.

QUESTION TO EXPLORE
What is hindering you from sharing the gospel?

TEACHING AIM
To lead the class to describe the lengths to which the gospel had reached from Acts 1:8 to the conclusion of Acts, and to decide that they too will let nothing hinder them from sharing the gospel

LESSON THIRTEEN

Let Nothing Hinder You

BIBLE COMMENTS

Understanding the Context

When writing to Roman Christians from Corinth around A.D. 57, Paul expressed his desire and intent to visit Rome (Romans 1:11, 13; 15:22–33). What is more, he wanted "God's beloved in Rome" (Rom. 1:7) to know that this was not a new development, for he had often intended to come their way but had been prevented from doing so (Rom. 1:13). Would that we knew why! At the time he wrote Romans, Paul hoped to see believers in Rome and be assisted by them en route to Spain. Before heading west to Rome, however, the apostle was first committed to travel east in order to deliver an offering from Grecian believers to "the poor among the saints at Jerusalem" (Rom. 15:24–26). Acts indicates that Paul did in fact make it to Rome (Acts 28:14, 16) via Jerusalem (Acts 21:17), but as Caesar's prisoner and not as a travelling missioner.

Albeit bound, Paul believed that "the word of God is not chained" (2 Timothy 2:9). It appears that Paul wrote his beloved letter to the Philippians from Roman captivity. In the midst of his confinement, the apostle was joyful. He derived joy from his conviction "that what [had] happened to [him had] actually helped to spread the gospel . . . " (Philippians 1:12). The gospel's progress, not his personal attainments, was his chief concern. From the time of his conversion, Paul's passionate commitment was to proclaim the gospel "in season, out of season" (2 Timothy 4:2, KJV). This lesson, which treats Acts' depiction of Paul's detainment in Rome, calls and challenges us to no less.

Interpreting the Scriptures

"And so we came to Rome . . . " (28:17–22)

Paul was a man on the move. At the conclusion of lesson twelve (Acts 17), he was in Athens. This lesson begins with Paul in Rome. According to Acts, after Paul left Athens, he traveled to Corinth, a strategically-located, heavily populated city located some forty-five miles east of Athens. Paul remained in Corinth for eighteen months (18:11). This would conclude what is referred to as his second missionary journey. Paul spent the lion's share of what is now known as his third missionary journey in Ephesus, a significant and sizeable port city in western Asia Minor. Acts indicates that he spent three years there (20:31). After some *toing* and *froing* between Asia and Greece, Paul bade the Ephesian elders farewell in Miletus, a seaport on the southwest coast of Asia Minor (20:17–38). From Miletus, Paul traveled to Jerusalem for the final time (21:17).

Not long after Paul's arrival in Jerusalem, an uprising occurred when certain Asian Jews accused Paul of bringing Trophimus, an Ephesian Gentile, into the temple. This uproar resulted in Paul's arrest (21:27–36). Despite Paul's offering robust defenses before both the crowds (21:37—22:21) and the council (22:30—23:10), hostility toward Paul was acute. Indeed, "more than forty" joined in a conspiracy to kill Paul (23:12–15). This, in turn, led to Paul being sent to Caesarea. There he was detained for two years under the governorship of Antonius Felix (23:16—24:27). Shortly after Porcius Festus succeeded Felix as governor of Judea, Paul— refusing to be tried in Jerusalem on the (trumped-up) charges lodged against him—appealed to the emperor (25:1–12). After a hearing before Herod Agrippa II (25:13—26:32), Paul embarked on a harrowing sea journey to Rome, replete with a shipwreck (27:1–44) and a viper bite (28:1–10). Despite the hardships, Paul at long last arrived in Rome, where he "was allowed to live by himself, with the soldier who was guarding him" (28:16).

28:17–20. Three days after Paul had arrived in Rome, he arranged a meeting with "the local leaders of the Jews" (28:17a). Knowing how the rumor mill works, Paul wanted to nip in the bud any injurious stories that might be circulating about him among the Roman Jews.

Paul's short speech (contrast 21:39—22:21; 24:10–21; 26:2–23) summarizes how he had ended up in Rome. Addressing those assembled as "brothers," Paul told them that he "was arrested in Jerusalem and handed over to the Romans" on baseless charges. He insisted he "had done nothing against our people or the customs of our ancestors" (28:17). Indeed, Paul reported that on examination the Romans were ready to release him "because there was no reason for the death penalty in my case" (28:18; see Luke 23:15b–16).

This fact notwithstanding, when certain Jews from Jerusalem objected to his release, Paul felt he had no other option than to "appeal to the emperor—even though [he] had no charge to bring against [his] nation" (Acts 28:19). Far from being against the Jewish people, Paul had called the Roman leaders together so they might realize his present captivity was "for the sake of the hope of Israel" (28:20). This hope of which Paul spoke in Acts is the hope of the resurrection (see, for example, 23:6; 24:15, 21; 26:6–8). This hope is grounded in the suffering, dying, and rising of the Messiah, who is light to both Jews and Gentiles (26:23; see Luke 2:32).

28:21–22. The Jewish leaders in Rome responded to Paul's defense by informing him that they had "received no letters from Judea" regarding him (note Acts 9:2; 15:23; 23:25) and that no fellow Jews had come to Rome reporting or speaking anything evil about him (contrast 21:21; Rom. 3:8). Furthermore, "the local leaders of the Jews" expressed their desire to hear from Paul regarding "this sect" that was spoken against everywhere (see Acts 24:5, 14).

"From morning until evening . . . " (28:23–28)

28:23–24. After fixing a day to meet with him, "great numbers" of Jewish leaders in Rome gathered at Paul's lodgings. There, Acts reports, Paul held forth "from morning until evening" (see 20:7). In doing so he testified regarding "the kingdom of God." This phrase, which appears only eight times in Paul's Letters, occurs thirty-eight times in Luke—Acts. As elsewhere in Acts, in this verse "kingdom of God" refers to the contents of the Christian proclamation about Jesus. Furthermore, Paul sought to convince his Jewish guests about Jesus by appealing to both "the law of Moses" and "the prophets" (see Luke 24:27). Whereas "some were convinced by what he had said," "others refused to believe" (Acts 28:24). Division is not uncommon when the gospel is proclaimed in Acts and elsewhere.

28:25–28. The resulting disagreement prompted Paul to appeal to one other Scripture as his Jewish dialog partners were taking leave, namely, Isaiah 6:9–10. In its original context, this passage was the message of judgment God gave Isaiah at the time of his commission to proclaim to

Israel. In the Synoptic Gospels (see Matthew 13:10–17; Mark 4:12; Luke 8:9–10), this text is cited to explain why people failed to comprehend Jesus' parables. Here, it is employed to help make sense of why (Jewish) people would willfully reject the gospel (see John 12:36b–43). Jewish rejection of the salvation that God made possible through Christ is said to be a point of entry for Gentiles who will listen (Acts 28:28; note 13:46–48; 18:5–6; see Rom. 11:11–24). (Please note: Acts 28:29 is missing from the most reliable Greek manuscripts and is not printed in the main text of the vast majority of modern translations.)

"Unhindered" (28:30–31)

In drawing his theological narrative regarding the life and work of the early church to a close, Luke reported that Paul lived in Rome "two whole years at his own expense and welcomed all who came to him" (Acts 28:30). For whatever reason(s), Acts does not narrate subsequent events in Paul's life. Perhaps the original recipients knew what became of Paul. Belated readers are left to put the historical puzzle-pieces together. Church tradition reports that Paul died a martyr's death during Emperor Nero's reign of terror in the mid–60s A.D.

In concluding his two-volume work, Luke was not interested in rehearsing well-worn details or in satisfying historical curiosity. Rather, he desired to convey the commitment of Paul (and the early church) to "proclaiming the kingdom of God and teaching about the Lord Jesus Christ with all boldness and without hindrance" (28:31). Whether in the first or the twenty-first century, whether in Rome, Italy, or Italy, Texas, believers in and followers of Jesus are to bear winsome witness "about what we have seen and heard" to everyone everywhere (4:20). We can do so boldly, if humbly, knowing that the gospel is "the power of God for salvation to everyone who has faith, to the Jew first and also to the Greek" (Rom. 1:16).

Focusing on the Meaning

Over the course of our study of Acts, we have been challenged to act on Acts 1:8. This programmatic passage declares that Jesus' initial and eventual disciples will tell the story for and about Jesus "in Jerusalem, in all Judea and Samaria, and to the ends of the earth."

Are we doing what Jesus said we would do by virtue of the Holy Spirit's empowerment? As we are going, are we engaging in holistic witness for Jesus, praying for boldness in our witness, and ministering to human need? In sharing our faith, are we willing to challenge accepted views for Jesus' sake, to be available to the Spirit to declare the gospel, and to offer the gospel to seemingly unreachable people? Are we willing to cross barriers to reach out to others while being faithful to share the gospel where we find ourselves? Are we committed to stay focused on the essentials as we witness in diverse ways to diverse people? Do we care enough about spreading the gospel light to overcome obstacles that may stand in our way?

As we draw this study to a close, recall the person or people who first shared the gospel with you. Are you not grateful that they did not shrink back from or shirk off this sacred trust? By God's matchless grace and empowering presence, will you join hands with other believers near and far to tell the story of Jesus and his love? "How beautiful are the feet of those who bring good news!" (Rom. 10:15).

TEACHING PLANS

Teaching Plan—Varied Learning Activities

Connect with Life

1. Prior to the class meeting, secure pictures of a running track, any type of boot, a snow shoe, and a pair of oversized clown shoes (try googling to find photos). As class members begin to arrive, show them all of the pictures except for the running track. Ask learners to describe what activity would best be represented by each of the pictures.

2. After the class members have a few minutes discussing the pictures, show the picture of the running track. Then ask:
   - Which of these shoes represents the best attire for running in a race?
   - How would any of these shoes help you win, or even finish, the race? How would they prevent you from winning or finishing the race?

3. Have a class member read from the *Study Guide* the Main Idea for this lesson. Inform the class that the shoes represent the things in our lives that hinder us from sharing the gospel (running in the race). Challenge learners to find what is hindering their witness during this lesson. Lead the class in prayer.

Guide Bible Study

4. Briefly summarize Acts 18:1—28:16, perhaps using the information in the first two paragraphs under "Interpreting the Scriptures" in this *Teaching Guide*. Then have a learner read Acts 28:17–20. Draw learners' attention to the presence of believers in Rome prior to Paul's arrival (Acts 28:14–15). Ask, *How do you think Paul would have felt on seeing believers in Rome? Had you been Paul, how would you have responded?*

5. Have the class get into small groups of four or five people each and discuss the following questions. (A copy of the questions is available in "Teaching Resource Items" for this study at www.baptistwaypress.org.) Allow four of five minutes for discussion and then have groups report their findings to the class.
   (1) What hindrances had Paul faced in his journey to Rome?
   (2) How do you think these hindrances affected Paul's attitude?
   (3) If Paul had done nothing to warrant incarceration, why was he arrested?
   (4) What made the Jewish leaders so adamant that Paul remain a prisoner?
   (5) Aside from being imprisoned, what hindrances do you see in the world today for Christians who seek to fulfill Acts 1:8?

(6) Is it a normal occurrence for those who are imprisoned to be able to tell their side of the story? What implications does this have for those who might face persecution for their beliefs?

6. Enlist someone to read aloud Acts 28:21–31. Have learners listen for how Paul spoke to the Jewish leaders. Then ask:
   - Compare Paul's use of the Scriptures here with his various methods of proclaiming the gospel in the previous lesson, lesson twelve. How is it different? How is it similar?
   - In your opinion, what was the biggest obstacle for the Jewish leaders? (Remind learners that Jesus used this same passage in Matthew 13:14–15.)
   - Was Paul's witnessing a success? Why or why not?
   - How difficult is it for Christians who face opposition to continue with their witness?

7. Have a learner read the small article in the *Study Guide* titled "Applying Paul's Message," and have the small groups (see step 5) discuss and report their findings to the included questions.

Encourage Application

8. Direct learners to the Question to Explore in the *Study Guide*. Ask, *What can this passage teach us about hindrances to sharing the gospel?* Ask learners to examine their lives to see whether these hindrances have affected their obedience to the command of Acts 1:8. (Note: Be sensitive to the possibility that some learners might not be fully committed followers of Christ.)

9. Remind learners that Jesus calls his followers to be his witnesses in their world (Acts 1:8). Have learners identify their Jerusalem, Judea, and Samaria, and record the answers. Write suggestions on a markerboard or poster paper. Have learners answer the following questions silently to themselves:
   - What things are hindering you from being a witness in these areas?
   - What things can you identify that need to be given up to be obedient to Christ?

- How can Paul's life give you encouragement to continue to witness even when things do not go according to your plan?

10. Close the lesson in prayer, asking God to grant the learners the courage to take action to remove hindrances in their life to being Christ's witnesses (Acts 1:8).

Teaching Plan—Lecture and Questions

Connect with Life

1. Prior to class, prepare a visual poster or collage that will illustrate some of the hindrances we face in following Christ. (Images or text might include family, money, personal goals/desires, the response of others.) Write on the board, "How can these items be a hindrance to a Christian?" Have learners consider the question while waiting for others to arrive.

2. Refer learners to the Main Idea for the lesson in the *Study Guide*. Explain that the purpose of the lesson is to challenge believers to identify and remove hindrances from their lives so that they may fulfill the command of Christ in Acts 1:8. Lead the class in a prayer, asking the Holy Spirit to show areas in which each person can deepen his or her commitment to Christ.

Guide Bible Study

3. Briefly summarize Acts 18:1—28:10, perhaps using the information in the first two paragraphs under "Interpreting the Scriptures" in this *Teaching Guide*. Read Acts 28:11–16. Make sure to point out that Christians were already in Rome and some of them came to meet Paul as he neared the city (Acts 28:14–15). Describe how that must have felt to Paul, and use a map to illustrate the distance between Rome and Jerusalem. Discuss the distance in relation to Christ's call to witness in Acts 1:8.

4. Invite someone to read 28:17–31. Then ask:

- Was Paul's method of speaking to the Jewish leaders similar or different to his tactics in earlier situations? How so? Refer to the second paragraph under "Paul's Second Encounter with the Roman Jews" in the *Study Guide.*
- How can you be a witness for Christ even when things do not go as planned?

5. Have the class turn to Acts 1:8 and read it together from the printed Scripture in lesson one in the *Study Guide.* Lead them to compare that verse with Acts 28:31. Ask, *How had Paul fulfilled the command of Christ to be a witness?* Give learners a few moments to respond, and then ask: *Where is your Jerusalem? your Judea? your Samaria? your "remotest part of the earth"* (NASB)?

6. Have someone read again Acts 28:24–28. Comment on the background of 28:26–27 using material on these verses in "Bible Comments" in this *Teaching Guide.* Ask:
   - What made the Jewish leaders so stubborn in their rejection of Paul?
   - How can rejection serve as a hindrance to believers who try to witness? How can it be beneficial to a believer? (Hint: see Luke 10:16–17.)
   - How is success in witnessing defined?

Encourage Application

7. Direct learners to the small article in the *Study Guide* titled "Paul's Name Change." Invite someone to read it aloud. Hand out slips of paper to the class and ask them to prayerfully consider the final question from the article. Have the class write their answers on the slips of paper, and keep the slips of paper in their Bibles as reminders to not allow hindrances to prevent their witnessing for Christ.

8. Close the lesson in prayer, asking God to give the learners courage in their witnessing, and to help them identify and remove any hindrance they might have written down.

How to Order More Bible Study Materials

It's easy! Just fill in the following information. For additional Bible study materials available both in print and online, see www.baptistwaypress.org, or get a complete order form of available print materials—including Spanish materials—by calling 1-866-249-1799 or e-mailing baptistway@texasbaptists.org.

Title of item	Price	Quantity	Cost
This Issue:			
The Book of Acts: Time to Act on Acts 1:8—Study Guide (BWP001142)	$3.95	_____	_____
The Book of Acts: Time to Act on Acts 1:8—Large Print Study Guide (BWP001143)	$4.25	_____	_____
The Book of Acts: Time to Act on Acts 1:8—Teaching Guide (BWP001144)	$4.95	_____	_____
Additional Issues Available:			
Growing Together in Christ—Study Guide (BWP001036)	$3.25	_____	_____
Growing Together in Christ—Teaching Guide (BWP001038)	$3.75	_____	_____
Living Generously for Jesus' Sake—Study Guide (BWP001137)	$3.95	_____	_____
Living Generously for Jesus' Sake—Large Print Study Guide (BWP001138)	$4.25	_____	_____
Living Generously for Jesus' Sake—Teaching Guide (BWP001139)	$4.95	_____	_____
Living Faith in Daily Life—Study Guide (BWP001095)	$3.55	_____	_____
Living Faith in Daily Life—Large Print Study Guide (BWP001096)	$3.95	_____	_____
Living Faith in Daily Life—Teaching Guide (BWP001097)	$4.25	_____	_____
Participating in God's Mission—Study Guide (BWP001077)	$3.55	_____	_____
Participating in God's Mission—Large Print Study Guide (BWP001078)	$3.95	_____	_____
Participating in God's Mission—Teaching Guide (BWP001079)	$3.95	_____	_____
Profiles in Character—Study Guide (BWP001112)	$3.55	_____	_____
Profiles in Character—Large Print Study Guide (BWP001113)	$4.25	_____	_____
Profiles in Character—Teaching Guide (BWP001114)	$4.95	_____	_____
Genesis: People Relating to God—Study Guide (BWP001088)	$2.35	_____	_____
Genesis: People Relating to God—Large Print Study Guide (BWP001089)	$2.75	_____	_____
Genesis: People Relating to God—Teaching Guide (BWP001090)	$2.95	_____	_____
Genesis 12—50: Family Matters—Study Guide (BWP000034)	$1.95	_____	_____
Genesis 12—50: Family Matters—Teaching Guide (BWP000035)	$2.45	_____	_____
Leviticus, Numbers, Deuteronomy—Study Guide (BWP000053)	$2.35	_____	_____
Leviticus, Numbers, Deuteronomy—Large Print Study Guide (BWP000052)	$2.35	_____	_____
Leviticus, Numbers, Deuteronomy—Teaching Guide (BWP000054)	$2.95	_____	_____
1 and 2 Kings: Leaders and Followers—Study Guide (BWP001025)	$2.95	_____	_____
1 and 2 Kings: Leaders and Followers Large Print Study Guide (BWP001026)	$3.15	_____	_____
1 and 2 Kings: Leaders and Followers Teaching Guide (BWP001027)	$3.45	_____	_____
Ezra, Haggai, Zechariah, Nehemiah, Malachi—Study Guide (BWP001071)	$3.25	_____	_____
Ezra, Haggai, Zechariah, Nehemiah, Malachi—Large Print Study Guide (BWP001072)	$3.55	_____	_____
Ezra, Haggai, Zechariah, Nehemiah, Malachi—Teaching Guide (BWP001073)	$3.75	_____	_____
Job, Ecclesiastes, Habakkuk, Lamentations—Study Guide (BWP001016)	$2.75	_____	_____
Job, Ecclesiastes, Habakkuk, Lamentations—Large Print Study Guide (BWP001017)	$2.85	_____	_____
Job, Ecclesiastes, Habakkuk, Lamentations—Teaching Guide (BWP001018)	$3.25	_____	_____
Psalms and Proverbs—Study Guide (BWP001000)	$2.75	_____	_____
Psalms and Proverbs—Teaching Guide (BWP001002)	$3.25	_____	_____
Amos. Hosea, Isaiah, Micah: Calling for Justice, Mercy, and Faithfulness— Study Guide (BWP001132)	$3.95	_____	_____
Amos. Hosea, Isaiah, Micah: Calling for Justice, Mercy, and Faithfulness— Large Print Study Guide (BWP001133)	$4.25	_____	_____
Amos. Hosea, Isaiah, Micah: Calling for Justice, Mercy, and Faithfulness— Teaching Guide (BWP001134)	$4.95	_____	_____
The Gospel of Matthew: A Primer for Discipleship—Study Guide (BWP001127)	$3.95	_____	_____
The Gospel of Matthew: A Primer for Discipleship— Large Print Study Guide (BWP001128)	$4.25	_____	_____
The Gospel of Matthew: A Primer for Discipleship—Teaching Guide (BWP001129)	$4.95	_____	_____
Matthew: Hope in the Resurrected Christ—Study Guide (BWP001066)	$3.25	_____	_____
Matthew: Hope in the Resurrected Christ—Large Print Study Guide (BWP001067)	$3.55	_____	_____
Matthew: Hope in the Resurrected Christ—Teaching Guide (BWP001068)	$3.75	_____	_____
Mark: Jesus' Works and Words—Study Guide (BWP001022)	$2.95	_____	_____
Mark: Jesus' Works and Words—Large Print Study Guide (BWP001023)	$3.15	_____	_____
Mark:Jesus' Works and Words—Teaching Guide (BWP001024)	$3.45	_____	_____
Jesus in the Gospel of Mark—Study Guide (BWP000066)	$1.95	_____	_____
Jesus in the Gospel of Mark—Teaching Guide (BWP000067)	$2.45	_____	_____
Luke: Journeying to the Cross—Study Guide (BWP000057)	$2.35	_____	_____
Luke: Journeying to the Cross—Large Print Study Guide (BWP000056)	$2.35	_____	_____
Luke: Journeying to the Cross—Teaching Guide (BWP000058)	$2.95	_____	_____
The Gospel of John: Light Overcoming Darkness, Part One—Study Guide (BWP001104)	$3.55	_____	_____
The Gospel of John: Light Overcoming Darkness, Part One—Large Print Study Guide (BWP001105)	$3.95	_____	_____
The Gospel of John: Light Overcoming Darkness, Part One—Teaching Guide (BWP001106)	$4.50	_____	_____
The Gospel of John: Light Overcoming Darkness, Part Two—Study Guide (BWP001109)	$3.55	_____	_____
The Gospel of John: Light Overcoming Darkness, Part Two—Large Print Study Guide (BWP001110)	$3.95	_____	_____
The Gospel of John: Light Overcoming Darkness, Part Two—Teaching Guide (BWP001111)	$4.50	_____	_____
The Gospel of John: The Word Became Flesh—Study Guide (BWP001008)	$2.75	_____	_____
The Gospel of John: The Word Became Flesh—Large Print Study Guide (BWP001009)	$2.85	_____	_____
The Gospel of John: The Word Became Flesh—Teaching Guide (BWP001010)	$3.25	_____	_____

Item	Price		
Acts: Toward Being a Missional Church—Study Guide (BWP001013)	$2.75	_____	_____
Acts: Toward Being a Missional Church—Large Print Study Guide (BWP001014)	$2.85	_____	_____
Acts: Toward Being a Missional Church—Teaching Guide (BWP001015)	$3.25	_____	_____
Romans: What God Is Up To—Study Guide (BWP001019)	$2.95	_____	_____
Romans: What God Is Up To—Large Print Study Guide (BWP001020)	$3.15	_____	_____
Romans: What God Is Up To—Teaching Guide (BWP001021)	$3.45	_____	_____
The Corinthian Letters—Study Guide (BWP001121)	$3.55	_____	_____
The Corinthian Letters—Large Print Study Guide (BWP001122)	$4.25	_____	_____
The Corinthian Letters—Teaching Guide (BWP001123)	$4.95	_____	_____
Galatians and 1&2 Thessalonians—Study Guide (BWP001080)	$3.55	_____	_____
Galatians and 1&2 Thessalonians—Large Print Study Guide (BWP001081)	$3.95	_____	_____
Galatians and 1&2 Thessalonians—Teaching Guide (BWP001082)	$3.95	_____	_____
1, 2 Timothy, Titus, Philemon—Study Guide (BWP000092)	$2.75	_____	_____
1, 2 Timothy, Titus, Philemon—Teaching Guide (BWP000093)	$3.25	_____	_____
Letters of James and John—Study Guide (BWP001101)	$3.55	_____	_____
Letters of James and John—Large Print Study Guide (BWP001102)	$3.95	_____	_____
Letters of James and John—Teaching Guide (BWP001103)	$4.25	_____	_____

Coming for use beginning December 2012

Item	Price		
The Gospel of Mark: People Responding to Jesus—Study Guide (BWP001147)	$3.95	_____	_____
The Gospel of Mark: People Responding to Jesus—Large Print Study Guide (BWP001148)	$4.25	_____	_____
The Gospel of Mark: People Responding to Jesus—Teaching Guide (BWP001149)	$4.95	_____	_____

Standard (UPS/Mail) Shipping Charges*

Order Value	Shipping charge**	Order Value	Shipping charge**
$.01—$9.99	$6.50	$160.00—$199.99	$24.00
$10.00—$19.99	$8.50	$200.00—$249.99	$28.00
$20.00—$39.99	$9.50	$250.00—$299.99	$30.00
$40.00—$59.99	$10.50	$300.00—$349.99	$34.00
$60.00—$79.99	$11.50	$350.00—$399.99	$42.00
$80.00—$99.99	$12.50	$400.00—$499.99	$50.00
$100.00—$129.99	$15.00	$500.00—$599.99	$60.00
$130.00—$159.99	$20.00	$600.00—$799.99	$72.00**

Cost
of items (Order value) _____

Shipping charges
(see chart*) _____

TOTAL _____

*Plus, applicable taxes for individuals and other taxable entities (not churches) within Texas will be added. Please call 1-866-249-1799 if the exact amount is needed prior to ordering.

**For order values $800.00 and above, please call 1-866-249-1799 or check www.baptistwaypress.org

Please allow three weeks for standard delivery. For express shipping service: Call 1-866-249-1799 for information on additional charges.

YOUR NAME _____

PHONE _____

YOUR CHURCH _____

DATE ORDERED _____

SHIPPING ADDRESS _____

CITY _____

STATE _____ ZIP CODE _____

E-MAIL _____

MAIL this form with your check for the total amount to
BAPTISTWAY PRESS, Baptist General Convention of Texas,
333 North Washington, Dallas, TX 75246-1798
(Make checks to "Baptist Executive Board.")

OR, **FAX** your order anytime to: 214-828-5376, and we will bill you.

OR, **CALL** your order toll-free: 1-866-249-1799
(M-Fri 8:30 a.m.-5:00 p.m. central time), and we will bill you.

OR, **E-MAIL** your order to our internet e-mail address:
baptistway@texasbaptists.org, and we will bill you.

OR, **ORDER ONLINE** at www.baptistwaypress.org.

We look forward to receiving your order! Thank you!